A Family
Affair

A Family Affair

When
School
Troubles
Come
Home

Curt Dudley-Marling

Heinemann
Portsmouth, NH

Heinemann
A division of Reed Elsevier Inc.
361 Hanover Street
Portsmouth, NH 03801–3912
www.heinemann.com

Offices and agents throughout the world

Library of Congress Cataloging-in-Publication Data
Dudley-Marling, Curt.
    A family affair : when school troubles come home / Curt Dudley-Marling.
        p.   cm.
    Includes bibliographical references.
    ISBN 0-325-00101-4
    1. Learning disabled children—Education—United States—Case studies.
2. Problem children—Education—United States—Case studies.   3. Home and school—United States—Case studies.   4. Parents—United States—Interviews.
I. Title.
LC4705 .D83   2000
371.92′6—dc21   00-037005

Editor: William Varner
Production coordinator: Elizabeth Valway
Production service: Denise Botelho, Colophon
Cover design: Joni Doherty Design
Manufacturing: Louise Richardson

Printed in the United States of America on acid-free paper
04   03   02   01   00   DA   1   2   3   4   5

To my dad, who died soon after I started writing this book.
I miss him very much.

And to Ian, my son, whose life was threatened by a brain tumor
as I was finishing this book. All indications are that Ian
is going to live a long, healthy life.

Contents

A Family
Affair

Chapter One

Things Only Go Wrong for Other People's Children
Anne's Story

I am a professor of education at Boston College. I am also an author, researcher, teacher educator, and journal editor whose work focuses mainly on children for whom school learning is sometimes a struggle. I have been a teacher of students with learning disabilities and children who are developmentally delayed. I have taught in a third-grade classroom that included students who struggled academically (see Dudley-Marling 1997). In my professional life, I have learned to appreciate the important role parents can play in their children's schooling and I have, in my writing, encouraged other educators to find ways to involve parents in their children's schoolwork (Dudley-Marling and Rosenberg 1984; Rhodes and Dudley-Marling 1996). I have, however, also seen the ways schooling can become an unwelcome intrusion in the lives of families, especially for families whose children have been labelled "exceptional."

This is a book about how the lives of a group of parents I interviewed—all of whom have children for whom school is a struggle—have been affected by their children's schooling. My principal audience for this book is teachers who I believe will benefit from a better understanding of the effects of school trouble on the lives of families. Parents who read this book may take comfort in the stories of other parents whose lives have been affected by their children's struggles in school.

My interest in the effect of school troubles on the lives of families would seem to be a logical extension of my work with students who struggle in school; however, my primary interest in this topic is personal.

Besides being a professional educator, I am also a parent who has experienced firsthand the pain and frustration of having a child who struggles in school. As a parent, I have learned that even relatively minor problems in school can have far-reaching consequences for family life. For this reason, I have chosen to situate my discussion of how the families I interviewed experienced their children's schooling within the context of my own experience with school trouble which, as it turned out, foreshadows the themes that organize this book.

Of course, how my wife and I experienced our daughter's schooling is part of the larger story of our life as a family and our hopes and aspirations for our children. It is within this broader context of our hopes and aspirations for our daughter, Anne, that I begin by sharing *our* story. The following excerpt from a journal my wife and I kept for Anne during the first eighteen months of her life provides a good starting point for talking about the effects of school trouble on my family.

Anne's Birth: Expecting the Best

Dear Anne,

We've decided to keep a journal for you. This rather long first entry is about yesterday, September 28, 1982, the day you were born.

Chris's labor was long and difficult. We arrived at the hospital Monday evening and, by Tuesday afternoon, Chris and I were tired and discouraged. Then, early Tuesday evening, we were told that you— our first child—might be in distress, but we'd have to "wait and see." In the meantime, we had to endure a fetal heart monitor, which was strapped to your mother's abdomen. This machine produced a continuous readout of your heartbeat, which gave us plenty to worry about. By 8:00 it was apparent you were in serious trouble and the doctor ordered Chris moved to the delivery room "double quick," as she put it. Since you were "already in the birth canal," the doctor used forceps to pull you out. And, boy, did she ever pull. With one foot braced against the operating table for leverage, she nearly pulled Chris off the table. It didn't take long before we learned what the problem was. The umbilical cord was wrapped around your neck twice. The doctor quickly cut the cord and turned you over to an intensive care nurse who had been standing by. The nurse suctioned your mouth, gave you oxygen, and cleaned you up. The medical staff told us you had been without oxygen for some undetermined length of time and had been in danger of your life. But, within a few minutes, all your vital signs looked good and we breathed a sigh of relief.

Still, having feared the worst, Chris and I were in a state of shock. It must have been 5–10 minutes before either of us even thought to ask the predictable, "Is it a girl or a boy?" Within a very short time I carried you down to intensive care—you in one arm, and an oxygen tube that I held under your nose, in the other—where you spent the night. I've never been so frightened in my life. Then, while I was in the intensive care nursery, I was given a message to rush to the recovery room because Chris was in trouble. It turned out that she had hemorrhaged and lost two units of blood, but her condition had stabilized by the time I arrived. Exhausted, I left Chris in the recovery room around 10:30. I cried all the way home. I called my dad to give him the news, but I couldn't stop crying. Eventually, I had a couple of glasses of wine and cried myself to sleep. While I was sleeping a nurse brought you to Chris to breast-feed. We're hopeful. . . .

—(Anne's journal, September 29, 1982)

This isn't how I imagined the birth of Anne, our first child. Like most parents, I expected that Chris would be awakened in the middle of the night by *mild* contractions (we knew that babies *always* came around 3:00 in the morning), we'd get dressed, grab the suitcase we'd already packed, and drive to the hospital where, several hours later, Chris would give birth to our daughter or son (we were pretty sure it was going to be a son). Enlightened by our childbirth classes, we took it for granted that we would avoid the sterile, technologically intrusive experience our mothers had when they gave birth to us. We were confident that the birth of our first child would be an intensely spiritual event unencumbered by the technology of childbirth. And, unlike mothers and fathers from our parents' generation, we would experience the transformation from husband and wife to mother and father together.

We did experience Anne's birth together (when my wife read this part she reminded me that, although the nurses frequently expressed their concern that I eat to keep up *my* strength, the pain was all *hers*), but, as my entry in Anne's journal makes clear, nothing else unfolded as we had imagined. And it wasn't that we weren't prepared for the possibility that things could go wrong. We were well aware just how wrong things could go at birth. Up to the time Anne was born, Chris and I had spent the bulk of our professional careers teaching students with developmental disabilities and, for many of these students, mental and physical disabilities could be traced to birth trauma. Additionally, Debbie, the woman who taught our childbirth classes, routinely reminded expectant parents that even *normal* births were often complicated. We *knew* what could happen. We were, however, just as sure these things happened only to other people.

We were also aware that Anne's traumatic birth put her at risk for a range of disabilities, so we actively searched for evidence that Anne was OK and we were easily alarmed by any sign of a problem. I will never forget the day—exactly one week after Anne's birth—when Marilyn, one of the secretaries in my department at the University of Colorado, interrupted an undergraduate class I was teaching to tell me that Chris was trying to reach me because "there seemed to be something wrong with Anne." Marilyn insisted that I dismiss my class and call my wife "immediately," which I did.

Chris, who had extensive training in the treatment of children with cerebral palsy, had been unable to elicit a particular reflex in Anne which she took as a possible indication of cerebral palsy. In less than an hour I met my wife at the office of Larry Waldman, our daughter's pediatrician. Dr. Waldman also observed in Anne either an unwillingness or an inability to use her right arm. He agreed that this could indicate a neurological problem, although it was, as he was quick to point out, "too early" to diagnose cerebral palsy. "We will just have to wait and see," he told us. Dr. Waldman also ordered an X ray of Anne's collarbone on the chance that the routine check for a broken collarbone at the hospital had missed something. Every parent knows how long the thirty minutes we waited for the results of the X ray lasted. It's also easy to imagine our joy—and relief—when Dr. Waldman caught our eye as he walked toward the waiting area and communicated the results of the X ray to us by pantomiming the breaking of a stick. As I'm writing this chapter, I have lived on this earth for more than fifty years and two of the most emotional moments in my life occurred within the space of a week.

Once again, we felt that we had dodged the proverbial bullet. We no longer feared the worst and, as Anne developed, even our smallest worries evaporated. Before the end of her tenth month Anne took her first steps and uttered her first word ("doggie," not "daddy" as I might have hoped). She had just turned two when she told me, "I have a lot of important work to do" as she helped with the housework. On that September morning in 1988, when we waited at the corner for the yellow school bus that would carry Anne—our clever, sociable, and highly verbal daughter—to the school where she would begin first grade, we had few doubts that everything was going to be fine.

First Grade: Signs of Trouble

Anne boarded the school bus happily each morning and every night she'd spend literally hours telling us all about school, especially her new friend, Lisa, who had just moved to Toronto from South Africa. Anne was happy and so were we. After all, school trouble only happened to other people's children.

The first sign that all was not well came in late November during a parent-teacher conference with Anne's first-grade teacher. As her teacher put it, Anne was "happy, likeable, but *young*." Anne's teacher didn't specify any particular problems, but the way she intoned the word *young* troubled us for days. In our professional lives we had often heard teachers use *young* as a euphemism for *immature, delayed,* or even *slow.* We began to pay much closer attention to what was happening at school and my wife, Chris, was nearly consumed by her worries about Anne.

In March, Anne's report card stated that "Anne is making *slow* but steady progress in the first grade program . . . and completes work *to the best of her ability.*" We were immediately afflicted with a kind of tunnel vision that blurred everything on the page except the words *slow but steady* and *to the best of her ability.* The end-of-year report card from the first-grade teacher reiterated that "Anne [had] worked hard and made slow but steady progress" and "It will be necessary for her to complete expectations in the Grade 1 program before beginning work at the Grade 2 level." In other words, Anne had not completed the expectations for first grade. After reading Anne's end-of-year report, Chris was so distraught over "Anne's future" that she didn't sleep for days. "Anne can't read," she said. "They're going to put her in special education." "We should have kept her in kindergarten another year." "What's going to happen to Anne when she grows up?" "It's your fault." "It's the fault of the doctor who delivered Anne." "It's my fault." For my part, I played the role of the optimistic father who wanted everything to be fine. "She'll be fine." "Anne just needs more time to develop." "Next year will be a good year." This pattern would repeat itself every time Anne received a report card for the next seven years.

We had imagined that Anne's birth would be spiritually rich and medically uneventful. Clearly, that wasn't how it worked out. We were also confident that Anne would do well in school despite our professional experience (Chris as a speech pathologist and me as a special education teacher), which indicated that many children do not do well in school. But those were *other* people's children. Chris and I had both done well in school and we took it for granted that our clever, sociable, and verbal daughter would also do well in school. We could not even imagine how it could be otherwise. But, whatever we imagined, Anne's school troubles continued as the following excerpt from Anne's first-term report card in second grade indicates.

> Anne is beginning to have more success using phonics skills to decode unfamiliar words. She often has difficulty understanding written directions in her daily work. She must read directions slowly and thoroughly and then think carefully about what she has read. Reading at home will continue to build her vocabulary and improve her fluency in oral reading. She needs assistance in selecting material appropriate for her level. Anne's sight vocabulary is slowly developing which is

aiding the fluency of her oral reading. She is beginning to copy written language to convey meaning. She enjoys dictating thoughts and ideas to develop a story and uses illustrations to further express her ideas.

Taken at face value, Anne's second-grade teacher's assessment of her reading and writing development sounds promising—she was, after all, "beginning to have more success." We suspected, however, that Anne's teacher was writing in a code meant to comfort parents *and* to alert future teachers to Anne's *problems*. Generally, this code is known only to teachers, but, based on our own observations of Anne's reading and writing, conversations with the teacher, and years of experience working in the schools, we read the teacher's comments to mean:

- Anne is able to sound out a few words and recognize some words on sight, but is generally unsuccessful reading continuous texts.
- You (Anne's parents) are going to have great difficulty finding *any* books Anne will be able to read independently.
- Anne cannot write continuous texts (she copies text and draws pictures).
- You (Anne's parents) need to do more reading with your daughter.
- Anne may not be very bright. ("She must read directions *slowly* and thoroughly and then *think carefully* about what she has read.")

It may be that we read too much into the teacher's comments, but, nonetheless, this *is* how we felt when we read (and, in Chris's case, reread and reread) Anne's report card. For the rest of the school year, we debated and quarrelled over the meaning of Anne's report cards and how we should respond. Was Anne merely immature or was she less able than her classmates? Did she have a learning disability? Should we have her tested? Would everything be OK as her first grade teacher suggested? Who was to blame? What should *we* do?

Although we generally disagreed on how to respond to Anne's struggles in school, we did agree that we needed to take a more active role in teaching Anne to read. Up to this point we had read to Anne (at least) every night, provided her with an extensive collection of quality children's literature, and demonstrated our own interest in print (our house is full of books and we read all the time). We had not, however, made any sort of systematic effort to *teach* Anne to read. This all changed with her first-term report card in second grade. We began by increasing significantly the amount of time we read to Anne each day. We also made more of an effort to draw Anne's attention to the print on the page by (sometimes) pointing to words in the text as we read. When the text was particularly predictable—and we made a conscious effort to read predictable books (Rhodes 1981) with Anne—we often pointed to a word and asked Anne to tell us what the word was. We sometimes asked Anne to read along with us, in which case we'd lower our voices when Anne was able to take control of the text and raise our voices when she stumbled, a technique called *assisted reading* (Rasinski 1989; Rhodes and Dudley-Marling 1996). To make it easier for Anne to read along with us, we often read the same book with her many times over a period of several days, a technique called *repeated reading* (Carbo 1978; Chomsky 1976; Rhodes and Dudley-Marling 1996). Finally, we told Anne she could keep her bedroom light on for an extra thirty minutes after bedtime *if* she spent the time looking at books. (I'm pretty sure that this turned out to be the most powerful factor in getting Anne to engage with texts.)

By the time Anne started third grade she was reading at least at grade level and, within a couple of years, she was a better than average reader. Despite her improvement as a reader, Anne's school troubles only got worse. Third grade seemed to go better for Anne, but her final report card contained the ominous warning that "Anne still has some problems that should be addressed." By fourth grade it was painfully apparent what these "problems" were. Anne had become a good reader whose "comprehension of material read [was] very good" and her "written efforts [were] growing in sophistication." However, according to her teacher, she had great difficulty organizing her work and, as a result, Anne often failed to complete her work at school. When she did complete her work it was often misplaced or lost so schoolwork often had to be completed (or redone) at home. And it was uncompleted work at school in the form of homework that had a particularly disruptive effect on our family life. Since Anne often didn't finish her work at school, she tended to have *more* homework than her peers. Because she was less organized than most of her peers, it also took her *longer* to complete her homework.

Homework was generally an unwelcome intrusion in our lives. Homework affected my relationship with my wife, my son, and, of course, Anne. Some nights Anne began her homework right after dinner and worked on schoolwork past her normal bedtime. When this wasn't enough time to complete her assignments, we'd wake Anne at 6:00 the next morning to complete her homework. Some evenings we'd end up embarrassing Anne by taking her back to school to retrieve work she'd forgotten to bring home. Homework sessions usually began with gentle encouragement, but the anger and resentment we felt—at the teachers for assigning so much homework and at Anne for her seeming indifference to the demands of her teachers—often bubbled over and we'd find ourselves yelling at Anne and each other. The explosion of emotion that resulted from the discovery that Anne had lost eight weeks' worth of work on her "major project" in fourth grade was not a proud moment in my parenting career. Nor can I even remember what our son (four years younger than Anne) usually did while we *helped* Anne with her homework, but he wasn't getting much attention from us. (I cringe to think what Anne and Ian learned about parenting from these interactions.) Homework gave us little time to ride our bikes, walk in the woods, fly our kite, or play fetch with our dog at the park. It is no wonder that some nights I readily accepted Anne's assurances that she had no homework or *forgot* even to ask if she had any.

When Anne was in fourth grade, a student in one of my undergraduate classes asserted that homework was a good way to encourage parents to spend more time with their children. No doubt some teachers feel this way. Yes, homework did encourage (more like *require*) Chris and I to spend more time with Anne, but it was not time anyone in our family remembers fondly. Homework was merely a way for the unpleasantness Anne experienced in school to spill over into our family life. It is probably for this reason that I learned to hate homework. When Anne was in elementary school I came to deeply resent homework as an intrusion into our family life and I didn't have good feelings about the teachers who thought they were doing us or Anne a favor by assigning it.

Marital Stress: Fighting About School Trouble

A friend of mine once suggested that living with another person was one of the hardest things most of us tried to do. I agree. Negotiating a life with another person is one of the most joyous aspects of our lives but, even under the best of circumstances, maintaining a long-term relationship with another adult isn't easy. The presence of children often adds to the challenge of maintaining a happy, healthy marital relationship as couples are forced to renegotiate their relationships to account for the presence of new family members. It may be doubly difficult to maintain a healthy marriage when *school troubles* become a focus of family relationships. This was certainly true in our house where the constant tension around Anne's schooling sometimes took its toll on our marriage. Since we tried not to yell at Anne—and we couldn't yell at the teacher although there were a few nasty notes—we occasionally took our frustrations out on each other.

Chris and I were rarely able to agree on how to respond to Anne's school troubles. I wanted to be patient and support Anne at home. "Give her some time and she'll be fine," I'd counsel. Chris favored a more interventionist approach: "Let's get Anne tested." "We should demand more from the teacher and the school." "Maybe Anne needs special education." "Do *something*." Out of concern and frustration—and without my knowledge—Chris arranged for Anne to be tested privately during the summer between third and fourth grade by a psychologist with whom she worked. To this day I have never read the psychologist's report although Chris tells me that Anne has "above average intelligence." Nevertheless, this incident was just one more source of tension in our lives.

Another source of contention was Chris's demand that I should have done more to move the school to provide more support for Anne. "Use your influence," she'd say, "Make them do something to help Anne," although it was never clear to me what I might influence the school to do. More to the point, although I was acquainted with the superintendent and the principal, I was loath to ask for any special treatment for Anne. However, when Anne was in fifth grade I finally reached the point where my own anger and frustration—along with the pressure from my wife—overcame my reluctance to "pull a few strings" and I attempted to use my influence with the principal and the superintendent to get Anne some extra help without having her labeled as "exceptional" (I'll talk more about my reluctance to have Anne labeled in a subsequent chapter). With the assistance of the principal we elicited several promises from Anne's teacher including, for example, to monitor Anne's work more carefully and to provide Anne with more individual support and direction in the classroom. The special education resource teacher also agreed to work with Anne on an "unofficial" basis which was common practice in this school. As it turned out, the promised support from Anne's regular classroom teacher was never provided although Anne's next report card was the best Anne had ever received (all Bs). Predictably, we grew hopeful. Her final report card, however, was mostly Ds, which made us suspect that the teacher had given Anne higher marks merely to get us off her back. Anne's life at school was not getting better.

The tensions in our household were the worst in the days immediately before and after Anne's report cards came home. My stomach was often a churning mass of worries for several days preceding Anne's report cards as I anticipated the certainty of family turmoil. For Chris, report cards certified that something was wrong with Anne, that we hadn't done enough in support of Anne, and that Anne's future was bleak. "She won't be able to go to college." "She won't even be able to get a good job." For weeks after the receipt of Anne's report cards Chris's anxieties dominated her waking hours and frequently intruded on her sleep. Fatigue brought on by tension and lack of sleep made things look even darker for Chris. I was worried too, but usually I tried to defuse the tension by striking a more optimistic stance (a male problem, I think). "Anne's going to be fine." "We just need to work on her self-confidence." "Lots of people who don't go to college lead happy, fulfilled lives." From Chris's perspective my reassurances indicated only that I wasn't listening to her concerns and the stresses on our relationship worsened. I hoped that we could avoid the stress associated with Anne's schooling by trying not to talk about it since these *discussions* always led to a quarrel. But the regular intrusion of schooling into our lives in the form of homework, report cards, and notes and phone calls from teachers ("Anne didn't hand in . . .") made it impossible for us to ignore Anne's *school troubles.* And the tensions over schooling spilled over into every aspect of my relationships with Chris and Anne.

I don't want to be overly dramatic here by claiming that the tensions that derived from Anne's school troubles drove us to the brink of divorce, although there were moments when this seemed at least a possibility. I can say, however, that, for periods of time, our home was not such a happy place, as school trouble regularly denied us the pleasures of a warm, supportive, and active family life. Recognizing the harm that was being done to our relationship, we finally sought the assistance of a marriage counselor (we were lucky enough to have insurance that paid for marriage counseling) who helped Chris and I to "reopen the lines of communication" between us. I think it was the marriage counselor who finally moved me to intervene directly in Anne's schooling. Our marriage counselor also helped me to acknowledge the stress Chris felt over Anne's struggles in school. Marriage counseling helped us cope with school trouble, but summers—which provided a two-month break from the tensions of Anne's schooling and gave us some space to rebuild our relationship—were even more important for us. The ultimate solution to the tensions of schooling, however, was moving Anne to an alternative school. I'll say more about this later.

A Loss of Confidence:
The Effects of School Trouble on Anne

From my perspective, the most serious consequence of Anne's struggles in school was the effect on her sense of self. As I was writing this section, I asked Anne to talk to me about how school made her feel when she was at her "old" school. Anne told me that, during those years, she didn't find school interesting. She had no reason to work hard, so she often did poorly. She said that, "I could have done well if wanted to, but I didn't want to." She blamed a particularly poor report card in fifth grade on a letter we had sent to her teacher (and copied to the principal) documenting her teacher's failure to follow through on any of the promises she'd made to us to provide individual support and direction for Anne. The poor end-of-year report was "getting back at me for your letter," Anne said. Anne also recalls a "chain reaction": at her old school, friends were more important to her than school work but, when she did poorly in school, she didn't have any friends, and then she did even more poorly in school. Anne is also quick to blame her school struggles on "awful teachers," "poor explanations of the work," and "unclear expectations."

When I pushed her, Anne finally conceded that her report cards often made her feel stupid. Anne said that she always dreaded report cards and our reaction to them. Homework books (a way of helping us keep track of Anne's school assignments) made her feel especially bad about herself.

> Only the stupid kids had homework books so, if I had a homework book, I must be stupid. . . . Because of the homework books the other kids would make fun of me. "Anne's stupid, She needs a homework book." The homework books made me feel that even my parents thought I was stupid.

Just being reminded of homework books was enough to make Anne mad and she stayed mad at me the rest of the afternoon. In our conversation, Anne also expressed some resentment toward her brother for whom school is "so easy."

My own sense is that Anne's self-esteem was devastated by her school experience. Over the years she began to take almost anything she couldn't do well as evidence that she was "stupid." By seventh grade she was walking around the house with her head down and her shoulders slumped. Making matters worse, her confidence slipped to its lowest point at a time when the social rivalries among the girls in her class were at their height. The worse she felt, the poorer she did in school. The poorer she did in school, the worse Anne felt and the more both she and her classmates constructed her as a victim. It was this vicious cycle that Anne referred to as a "chain reaction." If bringing Anne home from the hospital after her birth is one of my happiest memories, the image of Anne slumping her way to invisibility is one of my saddest.

Still, even in these *worst of times* there were hopeful signs. In seventh grade, for example, Anne gave a speech in school on the political and historical meaning of fairy tales that was judged the best in her class, winning her the right to participate in a whole-school speech contest to which parents were invited. The same year Anne demonstrated extraordinary determination and stamina when she and I rode our tandem bicycle on a two day, 210-mile tour—most of the ride in the cold, wind, and rain. She was also beginning to read widely for the first time in her life showing a particular preference for Holocaust tales. There was also no doubt that, despite her setbacks at school, Anne was one of the kindest, most caring people we knew.

The end of Anne's year in seventh grade was, however, one of the low points in Anne's life and in our lives as parents. Anne was virtually without friends at school and, worse, some of the girls seemed to derive pleasure from tormenting her. Her end-of-year report card—poor grades and poorer marks for effort—gave us little reason to hope that eighth grade would be any better. On her seventh-grade report card Anne even got a C in French, the one subject in which she had consistently earned As and Bs. The teacher's comments referred to "math and written language skills [that] continue to challenge her [and] Anne is encouraged to review these skills over the summer in preparation for eighth grade." (Our reading: Anne's going to be in *real* trouble in eighth grade). Our worries about whether or not Anne would attend college were replaced with more the more immediate worry: How is Anne going to cope with the demands of high school?

At the end of seventh grade we'd had enough. We'd seen plenty of evidence to believe that, under the right circumstances, Anne could do well in school. It was also clear to us, however, that Anne would never thrive in school until she regained the confidence that had seeped slowly away over seven years of schooling until she felt almost worthless. The two-year-old who had "a lot of important work to do" no longer had to the confidence even to try. We were even more worried about Anne's taking on the role of victim, a particularly dangerous role for young girls. Something had to change and we pushed Anne hard to consider changing schools, but, early in the summer, Anne refused to even consider the idea. However, by summer's end, after a three week vacation to Great Britain, Anne announced to us that she'd go to school anywhere *but* the school she'd been attending.

We encouraged Anne to consider transferring to the Toronto Waldorf School because of the reputation of Waldorf schools for respecting children. Waldorf education, founded in 1919, is an international movement and, because of the emphasis on the "whole child" in Waldorf education, the curriculum gives equal emphasis to music, movement, art, handwork, and traditional academics (see Uhrmacher 1995 for an interesting overview of Waldorf education). As we pondered over the decision to transfer Anne to a Waldorf school, I read that Rudolph Steiner, the founder of Waldorf schools, once said that "Children are God's gift to humanity." This is a central tenet of Waldorf education. If Steiner's aphorism betrays an overly romanticized notion of childhood it also suggests a respect for children as important people and childhood as a significant time of life. And it was respect that Anne was after. When we met with a Waldorf teacher to talk about the school, Anne asked only two questions. First she asked, "Where do the kids at this school eat their lunches?" At Anne's previous school, upper-elementary students ate on the floor of the gym, a practice Anne had found insulting. She also asked the Waldorf teacher, "Do you let your students read the author R. L. Stine?" Since Anne had read little, if any, of R. L. Stine's work, my guess is that she was gauging the Waldorf staff's respect for their students by testing this teacher's willingness to censor her students' reading selections.

In the end, Anne agreed to attend the Toronto Waldorf School even though, because of differences in cutoff dates, it meant a second year in seventh grade. After just one year in a more respectful school environment, Anne began to do better in school. Her confidence soared, she began to develop better work habits, and she was *much* happier. It is not my intention, however, to promote Waldorf education. Creating a respectful learning environment is not unique to Waldorf education. It has been my privilege to have visited many public and private schools across the United States and Canada where respect for children is a basic pedagogical principle. I also doubt that all Waldorf schools fulfill their mission equally well nor do I believe that Waldorf education is the best learning environment for all children. It is just that this alternative has worked well for Anne. Nor do I want to suggest that Anne's school troubles magically disappeared the moment she entered the door of her new school. Missing assignments continued to be a problem in seventh and eighth grade. Anne has just completed her sophomore year at the Waldorf High School in Lexington, Massachusetts, and she continues to do reasonably well in school. We still worry about her work habits sometimes, and because she struggled with trigonometry and logarithms this year we hired a math tutor for the summer. But we're hopeful that her high school experience will be successful and she will be admitted to a *good* college. But our experience over the past sixteen years tells that we shouldn't take anything for granted. High school and college are often difficult times for young people like Anne. The academic demands are going to grow, there will be more homework, and then there's sex, drugs, cars, and alcohol. We know all this from our own experience, but we still can't imagine things won't go well for Anne as she grows into a young woman. Bad things only happen to other people's children.

Clearly, school has not always been a pleasant place for Anne and our experience with Anne's schooling has led to frustration, anger, tension, and, occasionally, despair. Still, I am mindful of the fact that we have been able to deal with Anne's schooling from a position of privilege that has certainly minimized the impact of Anne's academic struggles on her and the rest of her family. Anne had an immediate *advantage* in school because the values and discourse practices of her middle-class home so closely matched the values and discourse practices of the schools (Gee 1990; Heath 1983). Sharing a common cultural background with Anne's teachers also made it relatively easy for us to communicate with them (Lareau 1989). Because of our background in education and our own success in school, my wife and I also have a good sense of what schools want from kids. This helped us teach Anne "how to play the game" of schooling (although Anne often rejected this kind of advice). Our professional backgrounds also enabled us to provide substantial instructional support for Anne's reading development when she wasn't learning to read at the rate the school expected. My own professional standing gave me a kind of access to the principal and the superintendent that few parents have although I'm not sure this always helped us with individual teachers. Waldorf education *has* been a factor in reversing Anne's fortunes in school, but this would not have been possible if we didn't have the financial resources to pay expensive private school tuition. As difficult as schooling has been at times for Anne, given a different set of cultural and economic resources the pain of school failure could have been much, much worse.

A Family Affair . . . : A Research Project

In the years since Anne entered first grade, many parents have shared with me stories of schooling similar to our experiences with Anne. I have listened as friends and acquaintances told me about how their children's struggles in school have disrupted their lives and, in some cases, threatened to tear their families apart. I've heard innumerable *horror* stories about homework that recall our own experiences. I've overheard parents at soccer games or skating practice tell each other about the tremendous amounts of time and money they were spending for tutoring, testing, and private schools to help their children when schooling went wrong for them. I've sympathized with parents who agonized over the decision to place their sons or daughters in special education programs. In my personal experience, schooling creates a lot of pain and aggravation for a considerable number of people even in affluent communities.

As I listened to stories from parents that illustrate the ways schooling disrupted their lives, I was mindful of the forces in our society that are demanding higher standards, more frequent testing, more rigor, fewer frills (to the superintendent of one of Canada's largest school districts, art and music are "frills"), more days in school, more hours in the school day, more homework, a return to tracking, and so on—all in an effort to reverse what some see as a decline in the quality of American schools. However, despite the barrage of criticism of schools by opportunistic politicians and media pundits, there is strong evidence that children today perform in school at least as well—and, perhaps, even bet-ter—than their parents did. This doesn't mean that we shouldn't want our schools to do better, only that claims that schools are "broken" have no basis in fact (see Berliner and Biddle 1995 and Barlow and Robertson 1994 for comprehensive reviews of the performance of schools in the United States and Canada, respectively).

Putting aside for now the question of whether or not the quality of education has declined, my own sense is that the intensification of chil-dren's schooling experiences and the narrowing of the curriculum that results when teachers are forced to "teach to the tests" (Madaus 1988) will only increase the number of students who struggle in school with a concomitant increase in the misery in the lives of many families. It's like the high jump. If you raise the bar the accomplishments of the most skilled high jumpers will become more apparent, but the number of high jumpers who fail to reach this standard will increase. A similar ar-gument can be made for raising standards in our schools. Higher stan-dards will highlight the accomplishments of the most able students— and may even motivate some students to work harder—but unreason-ably high standards can also increase the number of students for whom school is a struggle. Don't get me wrong. I'm not advocating low stan-dards for our schools. Certainly, I want teachers to challenge my son and daughter to do their very best. But, in a system in which the suc-cess of some is measured in terms of the failure of many (As in school mean what they mean because most students don't get them), where everybody is expected to do better than everybody else (McDermott, Goldman, and Varenne 1984), the rhetoric of school improvement of-ten has as much to do with creating more failure as it does with im-proving the quality of education for individual students. Put another way: "It seems that schools . . . must foster a certain amount of publicly identified success and failure because of their role as a sorting insti-tution in a meritocratic society" (McDermott, Goldman, and Varenne 1984, 392). My worry is that the natural desire of parents, teachers, and the general public to create the best possible schools for our chil-dren is leading many of us to support educational reforms that produce more school failure and make life even worse for children who are al-ready experiencing difficulty in school.

It was in this context—Anne's struggles in school, similar stories from other parents, and demands for more rigorous schooling—that I decided to learn more about the experience of other parents whose children struggled in school. Beginning in the fall of 1996, I under-took a study of how parents of children who struggle academically in school experience their children's schooling. Specifically, I wanted to learn more about how school troubles affect families and whether other families, like mine, found that school troubles often denied them of the pleasures of family life. Would they find, as I had, that school troubles are a "family affair"?

The parents I interviewed included married couples and single mothers although, even in two-parent families, some fathers did not wish to be interviewed. In all, I interviewed six single mothers, ten mothers from two-parent families, and seven couples. Therefore, my findings favor the perspectives of mothers.

Since factors like race, socioeconomic class, culture, and language may affect how parents experienced their children's schooling (see, for example, Lareau 1989; Purcell-Gates 1995; Valdes 1996), I tried to interview parents from a range of racial, socioeconomic, linguistic, and cultural backgrounds. My sample included Asian (two), Black (eight), and White (thirteen) parents. Five families I interviewed had immigrated to the United States or Canada. Two of the families were Mandarin speakers who did not speak English in their homes. Most of the parents I interviewed were middle-class, but my sample also included working-class and poor families—one single mother was receiving public assistance at the time of our interview. Several parents indicated that they had not completed high school (one mother quit school after seventh grade) and two of the parents I interviewed had doctoral degrees. Fewer than half of the parents in my sample had completed college.

The *struggling learners* I discussed with parents—whom I describe in more detail in the next chapter—included eight girls and fifteen boys ranging in age from eight to seventeen. Eleven of the children had been identified as learning disabled (LD) and/or attention deficit disordered (ADD). One child was identified as language disordered, another as gifted. Most of the children attended public schools although two were enrolled in private schools and two other families were homeschooling their children.

There were significant differences in the degree to which the children I discussed with parents struggled in school. Most of these children did poorly in the majority of school subjects and a few exhibited serious behavior problems in school. A couple of children were not failing any school subjects, but were doing much less well than their parents expected. What all the children had in common was their mothers' and/or fathers' perception that they were doing poorly in school and, although several families talked with me about two or more of their children who struggled in school, that interviews generally focused on the child whose school difficulties were most serious.

Many of the parents I interviewed were referred to me by colleagues who knew about my research, and three families were known to me before I undertook this study. Six families were identified with the help of the director of a reading clinic affiliated with a university in southern Ohio. I located one family by placing a notice in a newsletter published by a private school. The two Mandarin-speaking mothers I interviewed were identified with the help of a multicultural consultant who worked in an urban school board. Four elementary school principals agreed to help me identify parents to interview, but this approach to finding parents did not prove to be very successful. In general, parents who learned about my research from friends or acquaintances were willing to be interviewed—parents contacted by school officials were not. In retrospect, this may suggest a general lack of trust in schools by parents whose children do not do well in school. It may also be that parents approached by the school did not trust me to keep our conversations confidential. I usually interviewed parents in their homes, though there were several exceptions. For example, I interviewed a Mandarin-speaking mother in the office of a school board consultant who acted as an interpreter for me.

In general, I asked parents to talk about the nature of their daughter's or son's difficulties in school and how their children's struggles in school had affected their lives. Some parents talked without interruption after I posed the initial question, "Tell me about your child's struggles in school and how it has affected your family." When interviews bogged down I would refer to my interview guide (Weiss 1995) which indicated some of the general areas I was interested in talking about with parents. For example:

- What is the nature of the *problem?* When did you first discover there was a problem?
- How have your child's struggles affected you and the rest of your family?
- How have you responded to school troubles?
- How has school trouble affected family routines?
- What are some decisions you've made that may not have otherwise been made?
- Have there been financial effects?
- How has the problem affected your child?
- How has the problem affected your relationship with your child?
- Have your goals/aspirations for your child been affected?
- How has the problem affected relationships with your spouse or other family members?
- Have these struggles affected your sense of yourself as a parent?
- How has this affected your interactions with the school/teachers?

I did not expect every parent to respond to all these questions. Ideally, parents told me *their* stories without much interference from me beyond probing for additional details. I referred to the questions in my interview guide only when parents were unsure of what I wanted them to talk about. Interviews ranged from forty-five minutes to one hour and fifty minutes in length, with the average interview lasting approximately seventy-five minutes.

Finally, even though I made every effort to interview as diverse a sample of parents as possible, I do not make any claims that the parents I interviewed are representative of all parents. There are groups that are not included in my sample. I did not, for example, interview any Hispanic or Native American families or poor, rural families. My sample also lacks geographical diversity since all the families I interviewed lived in Ohio or Ontario. Still, I am confident that the stories told to me by the parents I interviewed are not uncommon and represent some of the ways parents experience their children's schooling when school goes wrong. Each story I heard about a parent's experience with their child's schooling echoed similar stories told to me by other parents in my sample. The stories I heard from these families also recall tales other parents have shared with me informally over the years as well as my own experience with my daughter Anne's schooling. I tried to overcome the limitations of my sample by drawing on the work of other researchers whose work I cite throughout this book. In the end, I am confident that the stories parents told me, even if not necessarily representative of *all* parents in *all* places, are important.

This introduction attempts to describe briefly the parents I interviewed, their children, the nature of my research question, and the context of my own experiences as a parent from which this study emerges. In the rest of this book I endeavor to share my interpretation of the stories told to me by the parents I interviewed; specifically, how did schooling affect the lives of these parents when their children didn't do as well in school as they had hoped for? In Chapter 2, I share parents' narratives on the nature of their children's struggles in school which range from serious academic and behavior problems to doing less well in school than their parents hoped. Chapter 3 presents parents' views on how school troubles affected their children, including the mother who asserted that school made her son "miserable for six-and-a-half hours a day." In general, I found that school troubles diminished children's ability to find pleasure in their lives. In the next chapter I draw on the voices of parents to illustrate the sometimes devastating effects of homework on the lives of families. It is fair to say that the intrusion of schooling into homes in the form of homework was, perhaps, the most stressful consequence of school troubles for the parents I interviewed. Chapter 5 takes up the effect of school troubles on family relations and, overall, school troubles were a major factor in shaping family relationships. The burdens of school troubles did not fall evenly within the families I interviewed, however, and in Chapter 6 I discuss how the material and emotional burdens of school trouble fell most heavily on mothers, especially single mothers. Chapter 7 reviews parents' efforts to locate a cause for their children's struggles in school, particularly parents' ambivalent relationship with labels. In Chapter 8, I describe how parents' perceptions of their children were shaped by school troubles and, at the same time, how parents resisted efforts by schools to narrowly construct their children as "problems." If school troubles diminish the lives of families, it should come as no surprise that parents are ambivalent about schools, the institution that they hold most responsible for their children's struggles. Chapter 9 considers the complicated relationships between parents of children who struggle in school and the schools their children attend. Finally, Chapter 10 highlights what is the most important finding of my interviews with parents. The parents I interviewed cared deeply about their children and their children's education even if they differed in terms of the material, spiritual, personal, and interpersonal resources they could bring to bear in support of their children's schooling. I conclude this chapter, and this book, by offering advice to teachers and parents for dealing with the effects of school troubles.

The stories these parents shared, always interesting and sometimes painful, offer a cautionary tale for educators and educational policy makers. The effects of *school troubles* extend beyond the walls of the school and we educators should, therefore, be wary of practices and reforms that do not consider the effects of school failure on the lives of children and their families.

Chapter Two

The Nature
of School Troubles

At the end of first grade he wasn't reading independently at all. He was "reading" picture books that had been read to him. He had all kinds of advantages before he went to school. And he wasn't picking it up as quickly as we would have thought he would. Our daughter was reading before she got to school. And then along came Sam. He became an independent reader about fourth grade.

Interview with Betty Springs*

Through the eyes of their parents, newborn infants have almost un-limited potential for intelligence, wisdom, beauty, and athleticism. Reality, in the form of dirty diapers, tantrums, and sleepless nights, usu-ally requires that parents adjust – however slightly—their initial vision of their children as "tiny bundles of perfection." Still, despite the chal-lenges of parenting an infant, few parents doubt that they will be able to provide their daughters and sons with the support they need do well in school and grow up to live happy, fulfilled lives.

Of course, parents' optimistic assessments of their children are well-founded. Every child who enters kindergarten—with the possible ex-ception of the most seriously disabled—is as bright, athletic, and wise as their parents imagine. We only have to consider what preschool age

*In order to protect the identities of the parents I interviewed, all names used in this book are pseudonyms.

children have accomplished to prove this point. By the time children are four or five years old they are, in the eyes of linguists, functionally adult speakers. At this stage, children have learned the meanings of thousands of words. More impressively, they have learned how to combine words into incredibly complex utterances to fulfill a wide range of communicative intentions. They have also begun to figure out how the social context subtly affects what they say and how they say it. (A request to an adult or a stranger calls for a more polite form than a request made to a playmate, for example.) Given the opportunity, many children learn two or more languages almost effortlessly. By acquiring language, young children learn, without stress, strain, or conscious effort, an abstract system beyond the capabilities of the world's most sophisticated computers (Smith 1998).

During their preschool years, children also develop a sense of right and wrong, life and death, animate and inanimate, human and non-human, and important and trivial. They learn to walk, hop, skip, jump, run, climb, and swing. They learn to laugh and to make others laugh. They learn what they like and what they dislike. It's likely that the average five-year-old child, surrounded by books and immersed in media and popular culture, has a more complete understanding of the physical universe in which he or she lives than the average adult did a few hundred years ago. Each day of their lives, children prove their parents right: They are brilliant learners. Arguably, the achievements of the school-age child, however impressive, pale in comparison to what children have accomplished before they enter the doors of their neighborhood school.

Parents, unlike teachers, tend to view the bright, wise, and athletic children they send off to school each morning in terms of their individual accomplishments (Lightfoot 1978). There is no doubt that Catherine Wallace, whose mother, Tanya, was the first parent I interviewed, was, as her mother described her, a "very verbal preschooler, [who] talked early, walked early, [and] drew marvellous pictures at a very young age." When children get to school, however, their teachers are less likely to evaluate them in terms of their absolute accomplishments than their knowledge, abilities, and skills *relative* to other students in their classes (Lightfoot 1978). Catherine Wallace, for example, probably wasn't evaluated by her first-grade teacher in terms of her verbal proficiency, gross motor skill, and "marvelous pictures" as much as her ability to talk, read, write, and do math *compared* to the other students in her class at that time in her life known as "first grade."

Schools in places like the United States and Canada have been constructed as meritocratic institutions that are expected to sort students based on some set of (presumably) objective criteria indicative of children's ability and effort. As novelist Barbara Kingsolver (1995) puts it, schooling is "two parts ABCs to fifty parts Where Do I Stand in the Great Pecking Order of Humankind?" (58). For some parents, schools confirm their hopes that their daughters and sons are, indeed, the "best and the brightest." The largest number of students will be judged to be *average* by their teachers; however, a significant number of children will experience some degree of failure during their school years.

Increasingly, norm-referenced, standardized tests are being used to compare children's academic achievements to other students in their state, province, country—or even other countries. The distribution of students along a *normal* curve—in which a few students do very well, some do poorly, with most falling somewhere in between—has become a taken-for-granted assumption underlying schooling. This assumption is rarely challenged by teachers, parents, or even students. After all, most of us have come to understand the human experience this way. The "fittest" survive. The excellent excel. Schools may, as educational researchers David Berliner and Bruce Biddle observe, "conspire to make 'losers' of many children" (1995, 326), but I think most people accept that this as a "fact of life," the way it is and the way it has to be, however unfortunate. We've learned to assume that there will always be winners in losers in the human enterprise and this "fact of life" applies to our schools even if none of us want our children to be among the losers.

I do not believe, however, that this situation is *natural* or inevitable. It is possible to imagine schools without failure (see, for example, Glasser 1975), schools that evaluate children as their parents do—in terms of their absolute accomplishments. From an anthropological perspective, for example, every child learns language well enough to fulfill her social and cultural needs. From this point of view, language skills do not distribute *normally*. Similar arguments can be made for a wide range of human skills and abilities. Claims that language and literacy skills, for example, distribute "normally" are based on standardized tests that are *designed* to produce normal distributions. Test developers deliberately set out to construct tests that produce normal distributions. In fact, test developers will work with a pool of items (i.e., questions) until the items they select produce the desired (normal) distribution. Arguably, we have created schools that produce so much failure among our students because we *believe* that this is natural, not because it *is* natural. Put differently, school failure is a social construction. Politicians may blame teachers and even parents for the failure of individual students in our schools and sometimes this blame may be justified. However, in my view, the principal reason children fail in school is that the structures of schooling demand it. Students fail in school simply because it was decided in advance that some students must. It has even been argued that the presence of failure in schools is necessary to motivate students to succeed and certainly school success is defined, in part, in contrast to school failure. Natural or not, schools organized to sort students on the basis of meritocratic principles will—and must—produce a significant amount of failure. The fact that schools have been roundly criticized by politicians and the media for not failing enough students supports the conclusion that one of the principal purposes of schooling is to create success *and* failure. Let me develop this point further with a little thought experiment. Imagine what would happen if, say, 95 percent of students in a state passed the state achievement test(s) for any grade level. You might think there would be dancing in the streets, but my guess is that this sort of performance would evoke criticisms that the test "standards" were too low. Educational reformers demand high standards, but it may be that the only acceptable proof of high standards is a significant degree of failure. Given these conditions, it isn't surprising that the first serious challenge to parents' idealistic assessments of their offspring comes when their children enter school.

In the rest of this chapter, I discuss the range of school troubles experienced by the children of the parents I interviewed. Identifying the wide range of *problems* that can lead to school trouble will help to develop an argument I wish to make later in this text: Even relatively minor academic and behavior problems at school can lead to major disruptions in the lives of families.

"The Problem Started in Kindergarten . . ."

Since parents generally don't expect formal academic instruction to commence until first grade, it must have come as a surprise to Rosa Jones when she was told by the school that her son had a reading problem when her son was still in kindergarten.

> I think the problem started in kindergarten. [At first] I'd go to school every day and ask the teacher how he was doing. She'd say "Perfect. Lovely. I wish he was my child." And then when she sent the final report card—in kindergarten you only get two report cards—so when she sent the final report card, she said, "I think we should flunk [him]. We'll keep him back in kindergarten." And I said, "Well, why?" And she said, "He can't do his alphabet and he doesn't know his numbers."

Rosa Jones was among several parents I spoke to who indicated that their children's "reading problems" were identified prior to first grade. Mr. and Mrs. McIsaac, who immigrated to Canada from Ireland, also recalled that the first hint of their son Robert's school troubles came from his kindergarten teacher. Apparently, the teacher expressed her surprise when she discovered that Robert would be entering first

grade the following year (in Ontario children attend "junior" kindergarten at age four and "senior" kindergarten at age five). Here's how
Mrs. McIsaac put it:

> I remember Robert joined that group in senior kindergarten. I re-
> member it was toward the end of senior kindergarten that I said some-
> thing about first grade to the teacher. Because it was a combined se-
> nior and junior kindergarten class she thought Robert was in junior
> kindergarten, but he was really senior kindergarten, preparing for first
> grade. Then she came down heavy on him. . . . When he came home
> he'd tell me how, it was near the end of the year, she had to know
> what he could do. Like her field notes, her evaluation. And she said
> he couldn't write his name properly, couldn't count to whatever num-
> ber he was supposed to count to before he went into first grade.

These conversations with Robert's kindergarten teacher were the
first signs his parents had that school might not go well for Robert. Until
then his parents felt that Robert's overall development, especially his
gross motor skill, was superior to most his peers. But, according to his
parents, it was in first and second grade that things really began to fall
apart for Robert. As his father put it:

> First grade was a disaster for Robert. Just a disaster. . . . And then in
> second grade, I thought he was going to have a good time that year be-
> cause the teacher he had was very 'sporty,' but two weeks into the
> school it was a nightmare. . . . He couldn't read at all. That's why he
> couldn't do second grade [although] we didn't doubt he could read if
> he wanted to read.

Most of the parents I interviewed indicated that the problems
their daughters and sons encountered in school could be traced to "reading problems." However, unlike Rosa Jones and the McIsaacs, their
children's reading problems didn't emerge until first grade or later.
Mrs. Dumay, for example, told me that:

> Well, I think it started when Georgina was in first grade. . . . What she
> had problems with mostly was [reading] comprehension. At school
> they would read a paragraph, or read something, and then she had to
> tell [her teacher] what she thought [it meant], and she never could
> get it straight. She'd go all off. I thought maybe she had a hearing
> problem. That made me think I had to go to other avenues, more than
> just ability. I thought it was a physical thing, something wrong with
> her hearing. . . . But her hearing was fine. So, basically, it was reading
> comprehension, after she'd read something, telling it right back. Or
> writing it down. She couldn't write it down. She couldn't give the de-
> tails back. So that was basically . . . what most of her problem was from
> first grade on.

My interview with Mrs. Dumay reinforced my experience that
reading difficulties tend to be pervasive, affecting children's overall

performance in school. When I asked Mrs. Dumay, for example, if her daughter's reading problems had affected her performance in other academic areas she said:

> Oh, yes! Math, definitely math, social studies. Just about every subject because you have to read. So she didn't understand, she read it, then she would read . . . this is the second, third grade now, she should have been reading a little bit better than she was. She would pause after each word. . . . That's what they saw, there were some problems. She was slower, slower than they . . . that's what [Georgina's teachers] told me. Slower than the average child in reading and comprehension. Then the other subjects were affected.

Parents indicated to me that their children's early learning difficulties were usually identified by their teachers. Mr. and Mrs. Cooper, however, said that their son's reading difficulties were identified by district-wide achievements tests administered at the end of first grade. It was on the basis of these tests, the Coopers told me, that the school's decision to retain their son in first grade was based. This was very upsetting to Mr. Cooper, who was skeptical about the use of formal tests with young children. Talking about his son's experience in the public school, before he and his wife undertook homeschooling with their children, he told me:

> My son's difficulties started when he was in the first grade, and he was in the public school system. It started towards the end of the year. His reading was not progressing. He didn't have a behavior problem, it was more academic. And they started taking this test called Rubrics [a kind of outcomes-based assessment]. I had a lot questions about testing at the time. And when they couldn't answer much about why the Rubric test was so important, what was the reason for Rubric testing, because they also give what they call the CAT [California Achievement Test] test. I guess my question was: Why is there so much testing at such an early age? How will this affect my child? But he didn't score well on the reading. The teacher let us know that reading affects the majority of other areas, subjects in the classroom and, therefore, he would have to be held back in the first grade.

Trouble with academics wasn't always the initial indication that school wasn't going well for the parents I interviewed. Several mothers and fathers told me that reports of social/behavior problems at school were the first signs of school trouble. Betty Blake, a single mother, told me that her son's difficulties "started with some altercations he was apparently getting into at school with different kids and the teachers described him as being disruptive." When I asked Betty for an example of her son's "disruptive behavior" she described the following incident.

> In second grade [the teacher and principal] told me that my son, Timmy, was out on the playground. They have a snack time when

they are at recess and, if you forget your snack upstairs [in the class-room], you cannot go back upstairs to get it. That's it, too bad. Timmy forgot his snack one particular morning and so, when he was down-stairs, there was a girl who had a snack and he must have asked her for some and she said, "No." Now, I can only see my son asking a girl for some of her snack if, when he had his snack, she must have asked him [for some of his snack] and he gave it to her. So she had her snack, and he was hungry, he said, and he asked her and she said, "no." So he grabbed her. He grabbed her by the neck and started shak-ing her.

Betty Blake believed that Timmy's behavior problems were linked directly to academic problems, specifically to a school curriculum that she believed wasn't sufficiently challenging for him.

I indicated to them [the school] that maybe the reasons or the causes for his behavior is that his teacher's curriculum is not stimulating enough for him. If it's not challenging enough, or maybe he is not in-terested in the way that you are running your program.

There were moments, however, when Betty considered the possibility that Timmy's difficulties at school were motivated by a desire for "neg-ative attention," as she put it. Maria Scott also related her daughter Tiffany's acting out at home and school to frustrations Tiffany experi-enced with her schoolwork.

She would act out like I said, very badly behaved. She would tell the teacher what she was going to do and not going to do. I was getting phone calls from her teacher saying she's not listening, she's not do-ing her work. Then she'd come home, fuss, or get smart, which she had never done, talk back to me and things like that. And I'm like, this is not Tiffany because Tiffany's a happy child. And through that period it was like . . . and the teacher was telling me, Tiffany wanted to al-ways be right, always succeed. If she gets something wrong, she would get very frustrated and upset. And that would be with everything, not just reading, it would be with everything, something she does that wasn't right. So it was hard on her too. To where she would act out these behaviors that she shouldn't be acting out.

Other parents talked to me not so much about their children acting out in school as having difficulty attending to what was going on in the classroom—at least not attending to what their teachers wished them to attend. Catherine Conner, for example, had been told by one of her son's teachers that "in a classroom, even a custodian sweeping around a room will distract him." Two other children whose parents I inter-viewed had more serious problems focusing their attention to the de-gree that they were diagnosed as attention deficit disordered (ADD) and placed on medication (i.e., Ritalin). Celine Street, whose son had been identified as attention deficit disordered by a physician, described her son this way: "As far as difficulties of learning at school, it's not that he doesn't know how to do it. It's you've got to get him to listen properly. Because he can do anything. He can learn. [But] it has to be learned differently."

For many parents their children's early years in school did not trouble their assumptions that schooling would go well for son and daughters. For these children, school seemed to go well until third or even fourth grade before there appeared to be a problem. In other instances, there were no apparent school problems until middle school or even high school. And, if reading was the major source of difficulty for students whose learning problems were identified in the early grades, learning problems that emerged later were, according to the parents I talked to, usually associated with difficulties with "written language" problems or trouble with "study skills." Tanya Wallace, for example, indicated that her daughter Catherine's academic problems didn't become apparent until third grade. Her daughter had been slow learning to read, but had particular problems with written language conventions (spelling, punctuation) that plagued her through high school. Mr. and Mrs. Springs told a similar story about their son, Sam. Apparently, Sam had learned to read somewhat more slowly than some of his peers, but, in the words of his parents "he never really struggled" until he started high school.

> That first semester he had . . . science, history, self in society. All the subjects required that he have really good written language skills. He's able to express himself well in writing. Like if you look at *what* it is he writes, it's good. But where it falls down is on the conventions [i.e., spelling, punctuation]. And the expectation in high school is that anything you hand in is, like, a final draft. . . . And that's all they [his teachers] can see are the conventions. They can't seem to look past that to see what it is he is really saying.

For Sam's parents, a change in Sam's academic aspirations marked the degree to which things had changed for him in high school. His mother told me:

> Things really started to deteriorate for him around November [in ninth grade]. He said to me one time that, "I decided before I went into ninth grade, Mom, that I was going to work really hard and I was going to get on the honor roll." And he said, "Now I've just decided that I am going to work hard just to pass. That's what I have to do, just to pass." And that was tough for us to listen to.

Several parents I spoke to cited organization and study skills as the source of their children's school trouble. Edna Bunker's son, Mike, for example, did relatively well in school until fourth grade when he started getting regular homework assignments.

> Mike is a very disorganized person. He is an extreme perfectionist. He's got the worst qualities for doing his work . . . so it's been difficult because he would go to school and he won't remember what assignments he has to do. He won't remember the books he has to bring home. Like he's clueless. I keep waiting for him to sort of get it all together and I'm not sure that he will.

When I interviewed Mrs. Bunker, Mike was in eighth grade and she was very concerned about how he would do in high school when the demands for homework and studying would be even greater. She worried that Mike's poor organization skills would make it difficult for him to cope with the demands of high school teachers. Among the parents I spoke to, Mrs. Bunker was not alone in this worry. Disorganization was, perhaps, the most common concern expressed by the parents I spoke to, something I can personally relate to in our experience with our daughter, Anne. Poor study skills were also near the top of parents' list of concerns for their children. Mr. and Mrs. Mandel, for example, pointed to poor study skills as one of the principal causes of their daughter, Ruth's, school troubles. Mrs. Mandel told me that:

> Before exams I spent hours and hours with her. You know, show her how to study, how to make herself ask questions. When I asked her questions, she's to write them out. And then we review them. Help her remember things. Give her mnemonics, that kind of thing. Before exams we spend an awful lot of time with her.

For Elma Kinkead's daughter, Andrea, her problems in high school weren't due so much to studying for tests as test anxiety that interfered with her ability to take exams. As Mrs. Kinkead put it, her daughter "would completely lose it on the exam" and, in high school "they cover a lot on the exams" with the result that her daughter barely passed some of her subjects. Mr. and Mrs. Thibault also told me that "test anxiety" was the most serious problem for their daughter, Susan. Mr. Thibault said that Susan had to do very well on class assignments to compensate for poor test performance and even then her hard work often resulted in "barely passing" grades.

Not all the parents I interviewed had to wait until their children entered school before they suspected there was a problem. For these parents, early school troubles merely confirmed their early suspicions that their children might have some kind of "problem." Michelle Phills, for example, suspected that her daughter, Joy, had difficulty processing language when Joy was in preschool. Answering my question about when she first considered that her daughter might have a "learning" problem she said:

> With Joy I first noticed when she was in preschool, when she was three and a half. [The preschool program] was only for an hour and a

half a day or something like that and I noticed her with other kids and I noticed that she was much more creative that the average kid, but that she didn't really follow instructions. [I thought] that she didn't want to be slowed down by too many ideas or rules or anything like that. She was really highly creative. . . . And when I put her in kindergarten here in Megacity I'd ask her, "So what did you do this morning?" And I could never get an answer from her. If I asked lots of questions I would get little bits and pieces, but she could never give me any kind of overview. She and I were in a pretty confrontational situation for awhile. . . . I felt that she was holding out on me. And actually, one day I was, like, really angry with her, really upset with her. I was driving the car and I was so frustrated at not being able to get any information about what they were doing in school. And then it hit me. It hit me like a lightning bolt. "Oh no. She can't. There is something going on here. It's not that she doesn't want to [tell me about her day], she actually can't do this."

At this point, Mrs. Phills demanded that the schools test her daughter to determine both the nature of her language difficulties and the appropriate instructional adaptations.

Celine Street also suspected that her son had difficulties that could affect his future in school before he entered school.

With Dennis it really started when he was in day care. Believe it or not. When he was about three, one of his day care workers decided she didn't like something he was doing, so she went to grab him. First of all, do not touch Dennis. He does not like to be grabbed any more than he likes to be yelled at. When I got it from him, as much as a three-year-old can tell me what's going on, he was doing something that he wanted to finish and she was saying, "no, enough, it's time to do something else now." Because day cares are very structured—they have time for this and time for this—and when she went to grab him by the arm, he turned around and bit her.

Eventually, Dennis was diagnosed by a physician as attention deficit disordered and placed in a special class.

A couple of parents told me that, although they had no suspicions during their children's preschool years that their daughters or sons would experience school trouble, looking back, they felt that the signs were there had they been able to interpret them. Tanya Wallace, for example, told me:

I guess looking back there were signs that, developmentally, there were anomalies, I guess, things that she seemed to do very easily and things that she experienced difficulty with, that we would have never expected her to. And I guess we tried to attribute that to things like personality, temperament, developmentally, or she's on her own timetable, and tried to be very child-centered about it.

Similarly, Catherine Connor, looking back through the lens of folk wisdom she heard from other mothers, observed that her son, Max,

> could crawl about very early and walk about even at eight months and people always told me, "Oh Max is so physically active, you'd better watch out, he won't read." By golly, they were right. He rode his bike very early, maybe three and a half, four and a half. Somewhere around there. And he was just really a whiz—physically, but not academically.

As these examples show, there were substantial differences among the parents I interviewed in terms of *when* school became a problem for their children or *when* parents suspected there might be a problem. The onset of school troubles for these parents was, I think, related primarily to the degree to which school was a struggle for their children and the nature of their school troubles. For Mrs. Ng, an immigrant from Taiwan, school trouble meant that her daughter was placed in a special school for children with "language problems." For Betty Blake, school trouble meant discipline problems that led to in-school suspension and frequent phone calls from teachers and the principal. For Mr. and Mrs. McIsaac, school trouble meant their son's struggles with reading, part-time placement in a special education program for children with learning disabilities, and a general loss in enthusiasm for school. For Mr. and Mrs. Thibault, their son's* struggles meant consistently poor grades even with special education support.

On the other hand, Jamie Frick, Elma Kinkead, and John and Alice Mandel concluded that their daughters were struggling in school because they were "barely passing" one or more of their high school courses, although Ruth Mandel was also identified as learning disabled. Compared to the experiences of the Ngs, Thibaults, or Celine Street, it would be easy to dismiss the concerns of Mrs. Frick, Mrs. Kinkead, and the Mandels. After all, poor grades in a few subjects does not seem to compare to more serious struggles experienced by children placed in special education programs or children who have been retained, children who don't read until they reach third or fourth grade, or children who routinely fail (or barely pass) many or most of their courses. But, as the stories of the parents I interviewed indicate, even seemingly insignificant problems at school can have significant effects on the lives of parents and their children. Given my own experience as a teacher of moderate and severely handicapped students, a reading problem doesn't seem so serious. Yet, this is what a mother told me about the pain and frustration of having a child with a "reading problem":

---

*The Thibaults had more than one child who struggled in school. Most of our interview focused on the struggles of their son, Steve.

When you have a child who has problems with reading, you have something that's hurt, torn out. It's like it just hurts so bad you can't. . . . You try to do all the physical things you can do to make it work, you know, for them. But when you can't do any thing, it's. . . . Sometimes you can't do anything.

Other People's Children

In general, the parents I interviewed took it for granted that their children would do reasonably well in school. At some level they knew, of course, that many children did not thrive in school, but these things happened to "other people's kids." As Tanya Wallace, a special education teacher herself, put it:

> I think that we had always anticipated that we would be able to provide a preschool experience that would guarantee that our children would do well [in school]. It was a given. It really didn't occur to us that they would not do well. We knew that both our children met [developmental] milestones quite early. Catherine was very verbal as a preschooler, talked early, walked early, drew marvellous pictures at a very young age. So we were just went along thinking that school was going to be just a wonderful experience for her.

Mrs. Wallace's expectation that her children would do well in school was, in part, rooted in her own experiences with school.

> My dad was a teacher. He was a principal for forty years, but he never got a B.A. It was his expectation that I would be the first one in the family to go to college and my husband is the same. He was the first one in his large, extended family to finish high school. So the idea that our children would do well and go to university was a given. We were university graduates.

It seems reasonable for parents like the Wallaces to expect that, if they did well in school, so would their children. To the degree that intelligence is inherited, children's success in school is a function, at least in part, of their parents' school success. Even if there isn't a direct relationship between parents' school success and the success of their children—and there are reasons to question the strength of the relationship between innate ability and school achievement—it does seem likely that mothers and fathers who excel in school should be in a particularly good position to help their children learn how to "do school." For instance, not long ago, when my wife, Chris, helped our daughter study for a French test, she was able to share with Anne study strategies that served her well when she was in high school. Similarly, Martin and Betty Springs, one of the couples I interviewed, were able to draw on their successful experiences in school to offer their son, Sam, specific advice on how to improve his relationships with some of his teachers.

Not all of the parents I interviewed had positive school experiences to draw upon to support their children's education, however. For instance, Molly Reeves, an urban Appalachian, single mother, had a difficult time in school which, in her opinion, severely limited her ability to help her sons succeed.

> Well, I'll start with myself, I couldn't read 'n stuff. 'Cause I didn't get the help I needed when I was a kid. Both of my parents were drunks . . . so I didn't learn, but I made it all the way to the seventh grade. And I just dropped out. It was about four weeks after I was in the seventh grade. 'Cause I couldn't read or nothin'. I couldn't do nothin'. But I still passed all the way to the seventh [grade]. And then when I had Steve, my oldest son—he's 14—when I had him and he had to go to school and everything, still I couldn't read. I had to get people to read my mail and stuff for me. And I tried to read little books to him. I put my own words in them because, like I said, I couldn't read. So that put him behind a whole lot because I couldn't help him to do it right.

Despite what Molly Reeves saw as her own disadvantaged background, she was still hopeful that her sons would do better in school than she had. "I always tell them . . . be a doctor, be a lawyer, a veterinarian or something like that," she told me when I asked her about her aspirations for her sons.

Jeb Moore also told me that struggling in school was something he passed on to his son, Archie. As he put it to me: "I think part of it is inherited; a lot of his [personality] traits are my traits. When I was little, I couldn't read very well and had trouble in school." Still, Mr. Moore hoped that, despite his "inheritance," Archie would do better in school than he had.

The parents I interviewed all expected that their children would do well in school, even if that meant only doing better in school than they had themselves. Of course, schooling did not go as well for their children as these parents had hoped.

Again, my interviews with parents of children for whom school is a struggle made it clear that generic reading problems, math difficulties, poor organization and study skills, or "barely passing" grades can be as disruptive on the lives of families as a diagnosis of "learning disabled" or "language disordered." "It's just dreadful," is how Edna Bunker described her experience with her son's schooling. She might well have been speaking for all of the parents I interviewed, each of whom related to me the pervasive effects of school troubles on their lives and the lives of their children.

Perhaps the most significant—and painful—consequence of school troubles in the eyes of the parents I spoke to was the effect on the children themselves, which is the topic of the next chapter.

Chapter Three

The Effect of School Troubles on Children

Well, almost from the first day Debbie didn't want to go to school. She started wetting her bed, tears, wouldn't eat. Things completely out of balance. It was very strange and I'm wondering, what's going on here?

—Interview with Jamie Frick

My father was an executive for a large wholesale distributor in Cleveland, Ohio. When ruthless personnel practices—introduced by a new management team in the name of "efficiency"—created a high level of stress that denied my father the ability to find pleasure in his work, he resigned. As you can imagine, the stress he experienced from work spilled over into his personal life, affecting his relationship with his wife and generally making him unhappy at work and at home. Of course, my father was lucky enough to have had the financial resources to make the decision to resign his job.

Anyone who has experienced work-related stress knows the degree to which job anxieties can permeate professional and personal lives. Although it isn't always easy, adults who are unhappy with their jobs can at least try to find another job. For example, an adult who is unhappy with her job because she is unable to cope with the demands of her work—that is, she lacks the skills or ability to perform her job adequately—may be able to locate another job for which she is better prepared.

The same cannot be said of children who are unhappy at their workplace—the school. Unless they are at least sixteen years of age, quitting is not an option for them—no matter unhappy they are at their *jobs* of being students. Young children are required to attend school under penalty of law. Sympathetic parents, if they have sufficient financial resources, may be able to relieve their children's burden by moving them to a new school. Still, even if changing schools is an option, the demands of schooling—reading, writing, arithmetic—are relatively constant. People working in sales who find that they aren't very good salespeople may find a satisfying career in the service sector. An eight-year-old child who does not read very well, can't spell, or doesn't *get* numbers will not, however, be able to find a school where reading, spelling, or math are not required although they may find schools that value more than reading, writing, and arithmetic. And adults who find themselves trapped in unsatisfactory work can, at the end of the work day, at least try to escape workplace misery through various recreational pursuits inside or outside of their homes. In the case of children for whom school is a struggle, school misery often intrudes on their out-of-school lives in the form of homework and, as the parents I interviewed confirmed, children who do poorly in school often spend more time doing homework than their peers. (I'll have more to say about the effects of homework on the lives of these families in the next chapter.) Summer school, recesses missed to complete unfinished schoolwork, and after-school tutoring also limit the ability of many struggling students to find relief from their school troubles. Children who struggle in school may also find that their schoolwork is a major source of tension at home, interfering with their relationships with their parents and even their siblings.

Like most people, I recall my childhood as a carefree, happy time when I was untroubled by the complicated personal, social, and financial demands of living in an adult world. However, lacking the inner resources and maturity of adults to deal with stress and turmoil, children who struggle in school may not always have such happy lives. And, in the eyes of the parents I interviewed, this was the most significant effect of children's school troubles on their families. Their sons and daughters were not as happy as parents hoped they would be and, in the opinion of these parents, school troubles were to blame.

"He's Not a Very Happy Child."

When I asked parents how their children's struggles in school had affected the way they lived their lives, all but a few parents told me that the most significant effect school troubles had on their lives was that their daughter or son was now—or at some point in their school careers had been—unhappy. As Mrs. McIsaac put it, not long after her son Robert started kindergarten, "it was just like a light bulb being turned off." In her view, Robert entered school "vibrant and full of life . . . able to fend for himself . . . [and] lead his own learning," but then the "bulb turned off" and he became dull, listless, and indifferent to learning. Eventually, the McIsaacs took the dramatic step of removing both of their sons from public school in favor of home schooling. Even then, Mrs. McIsaac felt that it took "two full years" for Robert "to kind of become himself again."

Mr. and Mrs. McIsaac weren't alone in their assessment that school troubles had diminished their child's childhood. Edna Bunker offered the following evidence to support her sense that her thirteen-year-old son, Mike, "just isn't very happy." When I asked Mrs. Bunker to give me an example of how school made Mike unhappy she told me:

> For example, in the summer, he sat around all summer long and did nothing. He didn't go to camp. He doesn't initiate phone calls to his friends. He waits until his friends phone him. Then he decides whether he wants to play with them or not. I don't think he's a terribly happy child.

Perhaps Mike was just an unhappy child independent of his experience in school. However, parents were quick to make the connection between their children's unhappiness and what was happening to them in school. Susan Green's lament is probably true for almost all of the parents I talked to: "When my son started having school troubles, I saw a child who was really unhappy." It is no wonder then that Mrs. Moore told me that "the month of August, when it comes, I get depressed" because soon school will start, and, once again, her son would be "miserable for six and a half hours a day."

"School Made Him Feel Like He Was Pretty Much a Waste."

Writing in the 1950s, psychologist Abraham Maslow argued that human beings are motivated to satisfy a range of physical and psychological needs. In addition to physical necessities like oxygen, food, and water, humans have higher level "needs" including love, affection, belongingness and, importantly, the need to gain approval and to achieve competence and self-respect. However, according to Maslow (1954), people can become happy, fulfilled, and self-actualized *only* if they are first able to achieve some measure of self-worth. Although I doubt that more than a few of the parents I interviewed had even heard of Abraham Maslow's "hierarchy of needs," they nonetheless shared his belief in the relationship between their children's ability to achieve a sense of competence—what most of the parents referred to as self-confidence or self-esteem—and their children's overall happiness in and out of school. Janet Moore, for example, told me that her son's second grade teacher "just tore down his self-confidence." Single mom Maria Scott said that her daughter's experience at school "hurt her a lot because it made her feel that she couldn't do anything." I don't think anyone would disagree that it would be very difficult, nearly impossible, for any child, or adult, to maintain a high level of self-esteem when forced to spend a significant portion of their waking hours doing what they're not good at, in this case, *doing school.*

Many of the parents I interviewed documented their children's low self-esteem by pointing to their sons' and daughters' willingness to take school struggles as evidence that there might be something wrong with them. Sam Springs's mother, for example, recalled that when Sam was in second grade he asked her, "Can dumb kids grow up to be smart adults?" In high school Sam continued to seek his parents' reassurance that there wasn't something wrong with him by asking questions like, "I'm just average, right mom?" Carol Dumay also recalled that she often had to reassure her daughter by saying, "No, Georgina, there's nothing wrong with you." Mr. and Mrs. Mandel said that their teenage daughter, Ruth, had also asked them, "Is there something wrong [with me]?" In general, the parents I interviewed tended to agree with Catherine Connor that school had—at one time or another—made their daughters and sons feel like they were "pretty much a waste."

But my interviews with parents also indicated that some children were able to maintain some measure of self-esteem and contentment despite their struggles at school. Mr. and Mrs. McIsaac, for example, said that their son, Robert, who his parents described as "an outstanding athlete," was able to find satisfaction in hockey and soccer. Sam Springs was able to draw on his skill as a hockey player to feel good about himself despite his struggles in school. Sam even hoped that his hockey skills might enable him to overcome marginal grades to gain admission (and even a scholarship) to a college in the United States. Janet Moore, who told me that her son, Archie, was miserable "six and a half hours a day" also said the 4-H Club was a place where her son could achieve some measure of success (his parents showed me a picture of Archie holding a trophy he had won for the reserve champion heifer at the State Fair the previous summer).

Other parents indicated that their children were able to achieve self-worth and fulfilment through participation in nonacademic subjects and extracurricular activities at school. Catherine Wallace was, according to her mother, able to "find herself" through her love of drama and the opportunity to participate in school performances. Sixteen-year-old Ruth Mandel found acting in school plays and taking part in a theatre troupe places where she could feel good about herself. Diane Riggs' son Roger was also able to use extracurricular activities to create a happy space for himself at school even though he had serious reading problems. As Mrs. Riggs put it:

> Roger's a very happy boy. He likes to go to school. I don't have to throw him out of the house to get there. He joins in all the sports. There are lots of sports. It's a fabulous school up there and lots of things for him to do. He wants to do everything. He joined the recorder club and did well in that. He's on the traffic patrol so he does the traffic patrol after school or at lunch time. So he joins in and he's liked by the kids up there.

"Fabulous" schools like Roger's, Ruth's, and Catherine's offer and value a range of activities in which students, even struggling students, can find a place to feel good about themselves. Not all of the parents I interviewed had the privilege of enrolling their children in "fabulous" schools, however. Their children did not attend schools that offered art, music, or drama or provided after school programs that could give all students a chance to belong and, perhaps, to excel. Archie Moore enjoyed playing volleyball, but "boys' volleyball" was not available in either his school or his community. The closest organized volleyball program for boys Archie's age was in a city thirty-five miles from the Moore's home. Several of the children I interviewed attended underfunded, inner-city schools that placed little value on "frills" like art or music and didn't have the funds to support such programs in any case.

Of course, there is no guarantee that the mere availability of nonacademic courses or a range of extracurricular activities will serve the needs of all students. Joy Phills excelled in art, but attended a school that, in her mother's opinion, did not have a quality art program. David and Amy Thibault were even more critical of the art program in their son Steve's school concluding that the kind of art program offered in Steve's high school "killed his interest in art. Totally killed it. He'll never do art again." In the case of Mike Bunker, the chance to try out for his eighth-grade soccer team only gave him one more reason to doubt his self-worth. This is what Mrs. Bunker told me:

> Last year Mike tried out for the soccer team and his teacher was the soccer coach. Mike feels that he's pretty good at soccer and I think he's fairly good—I don't know, I mean it's hard to tell. But he didn't get on the soccer team and . . . Mike was devastated about that. I actually went in and talked to other people about that and they thought that it was too bad that he didn't get on because he needed that for his self-esteem.

Clearly, trying out for the soccer team didn't do anything for Mike Bunker's self-esteem. Unfortunately, competitive sports, like schooling in general, are organized to produce winners and losers and, in Mike's case, soccer was just another opportunity for him to feel that he was one of the losers. Still, the presence of a range of programs and activities at school at least increases the possibility that students can demonstrate their competence while they are at school. There is reason to worry, however, that recent demands for economically "efficient" schools with the concomitant focus on "the basics" (i.e., reading, writing, mathematics, science) will be used an excuse for slashing art, music, and extracurricular activities. The evidence indicates that this is already happening in many school districts. Many politicians and school board officials seem to have concluded that "basic" education is all we can afford. I would like to think that recent reports in the news linking art and music programs to enhanced academic success will lead to more financial support for these programs. My worry, however, is that taxpayers have been convinced that rich and diverse academic and nonacademic programs are no longer affordable or, worse, that such programs can only be offered in wealthy suburban and private schools in which case "the rich get richer." It is worth noting that Roger, Ruth, and Catherine, the three children whose parents said that they found ways to affirm their self-worth through programs like art, music, and drama attended either private schools (Ruth and Catherine) or a wealthy, suburban school (Roger).

We may have good reasons for demanding more from our schools, but, for many students, schools that limit their focus to traditional academic subjects can become joyless places that continually confirm their suspicions that there is something wrong with them. If we insist that children must spend nearly half their waking hours in classrooms, then we must be careful not to create schools that assault their identities as worthwhile, competent people. In other words, unless we are willing to accept children being "miserable for six and a half hours a day," we have a moral obligation to make sure that all children experience at least some degree of success while they are at school. This is a matter of broad program offerings and quality instruction, but children's success in school is also tied to institutional arrangements. Demands for efficiency and accountability, for example, have led to a proliferation of high-stakes testing and prescriptive curricula. But, from my point of view, norm-referenced tests that *demand* a certain amount of failure as a matter of design and standardized, one-size-fits-all curricula that construct school failure by making no room for individual differences (Ohanian 1999; Wien and Dudley-Marling 1998) are immoral.

Children are, of course, individuals and it's unlikely any two children will respond the same way to any particular circumstance. At least two of the parents I interviewed indicated that their children were "happy" despite their struggles in school. Diane Riggs, as I've already mentioned, described her son, Roger, as "a very happy boy" despite his academic difficulties. Similarly, Mrs. Tang, whose husband and son had moved to Canada from Taiwan three years earlier, told me that her junior high school–aged son, Edward, was having serious difficulty writing English. Still, despite her son's struggles in school and family tensions surrounding his school performance at school, she described her son as "a happy boy" and "an easygoing person" who was "quite happy with the program he's getting in school." On the other hand, Mr. and Mrs. McIsaac were among several parents who theorized that their child's tendency to be a "perfectionist" made it more difficult for them to manage school failure. Clearly, children's personalities were a major factor in how they responded to their struggles at school.

It may be that Edward Tang's "easygoing" manner helped him cope with his struggles in school better than other children. However, many of the parents I talked to shared their opinion that there were a range of factors external to their children that affected their daughters' and sons' ability to deal with school struggles. Mrs. Wallace, for example, talked about how the presence of a younger brother who was very bright and academically successful further threatened her daughter, Catherine's, self-esteem. She recalled a particular incident when her daughter was in fifth grade. She asked her mom "how to spell some simple word and Chet, who was in first grade, popped his head up— he's one of those visual learners who read without being taught how to—and told her the correct spelling. She just threw down her book with tears rolling down. This little munchkin [Chet] could spell it and it made no sense to her at all." I heard similar stories from several other parents.

While Tanya Wallace surmised that an usually bright sibling made it more difficult for her daughter to feel good about herself, she also believed that supportive and respectful teachers—and almost all the parents I talked to spoke of teachers who had made a difference in their children's lives—minimized the long-term effects of school failure on her daughter's self-esteem even if the effects on her daughter in the short term were quite serious (I'll say more about this shortly).

Just as surely as "fabulous" schools and teachers can mitigate the effects of school troubles, not-so-fabulous teachers and schools can aggravate the harm to children's self-esteem when school is a struggle. Catherine Connor grew angry as she talked about her son, Max's, second-grade teacher who, in her words, "humiliated him to the point where his self-esteem was at an all time low." Maria Scott recalled her daughter, Tiffany's, first-grade teacher who embarrassed Tiffany by regularly comparing (unfavorably) Tiffany's learning ability to her four-year-old grandson's skill as a learner. Still, parents who complained about teachers who, in their minds, tore down their children's self-esteem, almost always talked about other teachers who had boosted it. For instance, Cybil and Ralph Thorn, who were outspoken in their criticism of schools and teachers who they felt had harmed their sons, Al and Ted, were also quick to acknowledge teachers who managed to help Al and Ted feel good about themselves. Mrs. McIsaac, whose son, Robert's, "light went out" when he started school had a teacher in fourth grade who, in Mrs. McIsaac's view, had given Robert "the first year [in school] he enjoyed."

Some parents also speculated about how their own actions had affected their children's self-esteem. John Cooper shared with me his fear that he wasn't as sensitive as he might have been about his son, Peter's, school struggles—at least initially—and that this may have aggravated Peter's self-esteem. Similarly, Jeb and Janet Moore were certain that their decision to put Archie on Ritalin (a drug for controlling "hyperactivity") helped to convince Archie that there was something wrong with him. As Mr. Moore put it: "Archie's very sensitive and, like I said, [when we put him on the medication] his self-esteem went right down. He felt like we put him on the medicine 'because he was stupid.'" These guilty feelings led the Moores to discontinue the use of Ritalin after only a few months. In general, the parents I interviewed—especially the mothers—were very hard on themselves when they discussed their children's struggles in school. The tendency of mothers (but not fathers) to blame themselves for their children's school troubles was so pervasive that I take this issue up in depth in Chapter 6. For now, I want to discuss those children whose response to school troubles went beyond being *simply unhappy* to being depressed or acting out.

"Mom, I'm Not Depressed."

One day, "out of the blue," Betty and Martin Springs' fifteen-year-old son, Sam, volunteered, "Mom, I'm not depressed." Betty's immediate response was alarm. A year earlier a friend of the family, Winnie, about the same age as Sam and also having troubles in school, had taken her life. Betty was only somewhat comforted when Sam, sensing his mother's concern, added, "I could never do what Winnie did. I could never kill myself." No doubt Betty was uncertain whether to take Sam's "I'm not depressed. . . . I could never kill myself" as a reassurance or a warning. Sam may or may not have been "depressed," but, for a period of time in ninth grade, he worried so much over school that he couldn't sleep at night. Worrying about Sam's loss of sleep cost Betty lots of sleep, too.

Adolescence is a time when young people struggle to construct identities that make room for their growing bodies and increasing social demands and opportunities. Adolescents have a paradoxical need to reinvent themselves in ways that distinguish them from their child selves, their peers, and (especially) their parents, while still trying to fit in. Above all, adolescents need to create identities that allow them to feel good about themselves. This is all hard enough under the best of times as any parent who has experienced their child's adolescence knows well. It seems certain, however, that this is an even more challenging period in the lives of young people whose self-esteem has been threatened by struggles in school. I interviewed several parents of teenage children who told me that their daughters (and among the parents I interviewed only daughters were described as being or having been depressed), plagued throughout their childhoods by low self-esteem which parents related directly to school troubles, had been seriously depressed at some time during their adolescence. Speaking of her daughter, Catherine, Tanya Wallace said:

> She's not had an easy teenage passage. It's been rough for her. . . . I think this [year in eleventh grade] was the first time it hit her that math, no matter how much she studied or memorized, she was not going to be able to understand, and it sparked a lot of . . . she's had a very hard year. She's had a lot of depression, a lot of anxiety. . . . I think this would have happened . . . I'm surprised it didn't happen sooner.

Mrs. Wallace added that Catherine's hurt, anger, and depression had lasted through the summer, but that Catherine was seeing a therapist to help her get through what was obviously a very difficult period for her and her parents.

Although two other parents indicated that their children had been depressed at some time during their teenage years, this was not, according to the parents I interviewed, a common response to school failure. It may have been that Catherine was inclined to depression. Her mother did say that Catherine was "a very quiet personality . . . a very private person" who had difficulty "learning to be able to argue, to be able to disagree or not be perfect, not to say things that other people are unhappy with." Her mother added, "she finds it hard to come and talk. Even the doctors she's been with say that she's very withdrawn. She finds it hard to talk about herself and how she feels."

Perhaps if Catherine had a different sort of temperament—had she been "easygoing" like Edward Tang—she might not have fallen prey to depression. Still, among the parents I interviewed, Catherine's reaction to her academic struggles in school was extreme. But it is also easy to imagine that it could have been worse. Catherine had the advantage of supportive parents who had the financial resources to provide her with psychological counseling when she needed it and to allow her to attend a progressive, private school that her mother felt was unusually sympathetic and understanding. "I think that primarily the philosophy of the school has been responsible for some of her success because she's had a lot of opportunities to have quite a lot of support from faculty and to balance the areas in which she has difficulties with the areas in which she is very strong," Mrs. Wallace told me. Catherine was also fortunate to have a mother who, as a special education teacher herself, was able to provide some explicit support to help Catherine cope with her academic difficulties. We can't know for certain, of course, but the presence of these supports could be the difference between a young woman like Catherine who'd had a lot of anxiety and depression—but who, in her mother's eyes, was "coming through it"—and Winnie, the fifteen-year-old girl who committed suicide.

Again, my interviews suggest that depression and anxiety are not common reactions to school trouble. Teenagers whose despair leads to suicide are rarer still (although thousands of teens do take their lives each year). Still, I'm somewhat surprised that the parents I talked to described their children as merely "unhappy." I'm even more surprised that most of these children found ways to cope with their struggles in school, offering further evidence for the resilience of human beings. But no matter how well children and adolescents cope with school trouble, being miserable for "six and a half hours a day," as Janet Moore described her son, Archie's, experience at school, with constant reminders that they are less than adequate, is more than any child should have to bear. As a teacher educator and a former teacher it pains me to think that I have participated in structures of schooling that make some children unhappy for so many of their waking hours. For this reason, I believe that teachers have an obligation not only to provide the individual support and direction that students need to achieve some measure of success in school—which most teachers do well—but also to challenge the structures of schooling that produce such high levels of failure among our students in the first place.

"Acting Out . . . "

Many of the parents I interviewed saw a causal relationship between their children's academic difficulties and various forms of acting out and attention-getting at home and at school. Maria Scott, for example, made it clear that she believed that her daughter, Tiffany's, "acting out" in school and at home was the direct result of her frustration at school. Similarly, Betty Blake linked her son's acting out in school to "boredom" with a school curriculum that she didn't feel was sufficiently challenging and a need to "get negative attention." Unfortunately, his restlessness and attention seeking got him into serious trouble at school (recall the example in the previous chapter where Timmy got into trouble for "stealing" another student's snack) leading to frequent disciplinary actions including an "in-school suspension" in second grade. Betty offered me the following example of her son's negative attention-getting at school.

> Like in second grade he did have a number of incidents. I don't know what was causing them. I don't know, he might have been looking for attention and his own way of getting attention might have been through negative, by negative feedback. Okay. There was a girl that he liked, named Caitlin, in grade one. And in grade two he saw her again and I guess she wasn't really paying a lot of attention to him. So in order to get her attention, he hid some of her stuff. I mean this is seven-year-old kind of stuff, as far as I'm concerned. But his school doesn't see it that way. His principal said, "Well, why couldn't he have looked for attention in a more positive way?" I said, "He's seven! What does he know about looking for attention in a more positive way?"

Other parents also talked to me about their children's need for attention as a means of compensating for frustration at school although, in most cases, the attention-getting was fairly harmless. Tanya Wallace described her daughter, Catherine's, need for attention this way.

> During the years where she's just . . . covered up for the uncertainty and the anxiety . . . whether it was about school or social relationships or whatnot, she was, as I said, pretty bizarre-looking kid. If someone dyed their hair red, her's would be fire engine red. If somebody had her ears pierced, she had fourteen holes in her ears. It was like, "I'm really . . . I'm really cool!" And this real need to be recognized.

Jamie Frick had a similar perception of her then fourteen-year-old daughter, Debbie's, "fashion statement."

> Her clothing became very unusual. She didn't go into the Gothic stuff, it wasn't all the black. She found her own style. But all of a sudden, it seemed to me, that rather than wearing clothing, she was wearing costumes. She wanted to be noticed. The necklines plummeted, so lots of cleavage. Short, short skirts or no skirts. Tops over fish net stockings with the garters so that lots of bare legs from the bottom of the bum to the knee. . . . She'd spend 'til two, three, four o'clock in the morning figuring out what she was going to wear to school. That was the big thing. How she was going to do her hair. The hair started getting dyed, the second half of ninth grade in rather bizarre colors. It first got stripped down to a blond, but then it went fire engine red. She figured out that clothing dye, first she started out with Fun Dip. And that gave her a nice light tint on the other, so she could wear the tint of the day,

the flavor of the day. Then she found that Rit dye, she could get really intense colours, so it went fire engine red, then she put blue over it so it was purple. She wanted to go black. I said, "Wait." She was fourteen at this point. I thought this is still a little bit young. And she was doing things very intentionally to get attention.

To me, Catherine and Debbie's fashion statements seem like fairly typical examples of teenage rebellion but, to their mothers, this went beyond normal adolescent attention-getting and was a way for their daughters to either cope with or draw attention away from the frustrations they were experiencing at school.

The pressures of schooling may have also been a factor in Elma Kinkead's daughter, Andrea's, habit of skipping classes. Andrea didn't skip many classes, but this was still a serious concern for her mother, who expected academic excellence. Again, skipping the occasional class doesn't seem such an extraordinary thing for most teenagers. However, the lengths to which Carol Dumay's daughter, Georgina, went to avoid school when she was in first and second grade were more serious. When I asked Mrs. Dumay how school struggles had affected her daughter she responded this way.

> It affected her wanting to go to school. . . . She didn't want to go to school. Her stomach hurt. Her head ached. Something on my arm. I think, I don't know whether, I guess that was the thing that, for me to say, "Oh, well, then you can stay home." But I would never let her stay. I knew there wasn't something serious wrong with her physically. Well, two times I let her stay cause I thought maybe she is. It became too much of a pattern. I want to stay home. Can I stay home today? My throat is hurting, or my chest, or something. Any kind of an excuse. This is second grade now. . . . It seemed that every week there was a problem with that. Every week.

Mrs. Dumay believed that Georgina wanted to miss school so that she could avoid the other children who teased and made fun of her when she read out loud. "She was so afraid of what the other kids were going to say to her," is how she described it. Mrs. Dumay didn't want her daughter to miss school, but she didn't want Georgina to have to deal with the teasing that went on "behind the teacher's back" either. She advised her daughter "not to pay any attention to what the other kids say," but conceded, "it's hard for a child, I guess, when it bothers you so much. It makes such an impression on you. It's hard to tell to a child in the second grade, 'Don't let it bother you.'"

Sam Springs responded to the frustration of his struggles in ninth grade by experimenting with marijuana. His parents were alarmed by this development, but felt helpless. Mrs. Spring told me: "We went to our doctor because we just didn't know what to do. We just didn't. . . . We didn't know how to act. We didn't know how to deal with him. We didn't know how to support him. We wanted to kill him. . . . For him, I think, a lot of it is around self-esteem."

Betty Springs brings me back to where I started this chapter. School failure has devastating consequences for children forced to spend six and a half hours a day demonstrating their inadequacies. Among the parents I interviewed, low self-esteem made it difficult for their children to find much pleasure in their lives. Like Mike Bunker, many of these were not very happy children. For Catherine Wallace, her inability to cope with school failure led to serious depression. For other children, unhappiness due to low self-esteem may have been a factor in various forms of acting out and attention-getting including sassiness, physical aggressiveness, wild clothes, skipping classes, and drug use. Serious forms of acting out, like drug use and violence, were rare among the children of the parents I interviewed, but I can't help but wonder about the degree to which academic and social failure contributes to high levels of violence and drug use in some of our schools. Good students may also turn to drugs or even violence, but it isn't hard to imagine the frustrations of school struggles growing into anger or students turning to drugs in order to escape the pain of school failure. No matter how you look at it, the parents I interviewed indicated that school struggles were very hard on their daughters and sons. Again, this isn't so surprising. After all, as difficult as it must be for struggling students to cope with "six and a half hours a day" at school they also have to try to cope with the ways school trouble makes its way into their homes. Probably the most significant way school troubles find their way into the homes of struggling students is in the form of homework. This is the subject of the next chapter.

Chapter Four

The Frustrations
of Homework

*He spends hours and hours and hours on homework. All weekend
long, all night long. It's just dreadful. Just dreadful. It's been really
hard. . . . There's more to life than just homework and school.*
—Interview with Edna Bunker

Neoconservative Newt Gingrich, former Speaker of the U.S. House of
Representatives, has argued that "every child in America should be required to do at least two hours of homework a night, or they're being
cheated for the rest of their lives." (in Spring 1997, 16). Gingrich isn't
alone in his concerns about homework. Literally thousands of articles
and hundreds of books have been written on the subject of homework. Some of this work supports Gingrich's position on the value of
homework. Parlardy (1995), for example, is among those who argue
that homework teaches students discipline, expands the curriculum,
and increases student achievement. Other researchers claim that dif-
ferential homework rates are to blame for American students lag-
ging behind students in other countries academically (Walberg 1991).
Still, in general, the research does not indicate a strong relationship between homework and academic achievement for all students (see, for
example, McDermott, Goldman, and Varenne 1984, and Cooper 1989).
Homework does appear to positively influence academic achievement

in high school and, to a lesser extent, in the middle grades (Begley 1998; Black 1996). In the early elementary grades, however, the research indicates that homework has no discernible effect on academic achievement and may even undermine students' attitudes towards schooling (Begley 1998; Cooper 1989). Still, the relationship of homework to academic achievement is complicated. The quality of homework assignments and the ability of teachers to respond to students' homework are among the factors that influence the relationship between homework and academic achievement (McDermott et al. 1984). The indiscriminate assignment of homework can, for example, "exacerbate the sorting dilemma of our school systems . . . wreak[ing] havoc in a home and add to the number of failing children" (McDermott et al. 1984, 679–680).

Home environments, student characteristics, subject matter, and grade level also influence the effect of homework on student achievement (Cooper 1989). Families differ, for example, in their ability to support homework. Some families may not be able to

> observe routines or discuss school events, or even tell their children stories. They cannot provide books or supplies, and they do not have hobbies. Many parents do not know how to read. Many others work late. Most have little understanding about school deadlines or about how to "monitor" their children's homework. (Valdes 1996, 33)

Homework is a special concern for those who work with exceptional students, in particular how to improve the homework performance of students in special education who tend to have difficulty completing homework assignments (see Callahan, Rademacher, and Hildreth 1998; Salend and Gajria 1995).

Irrespective of arguments about the value of homework, it is likely that in any home where there are school-age children, some portion of most evenings will be devoted to homework. Depending upon the age of child, there may be a little or a lot of homework to complete each night, but it is taken for granted in most families that there will be homework. The sheer number of trade books dedicated to helping parents cope with homework—a few of the titles that caught my eye include *Homework Without Tears* (Canter and Hausner 1988); *Ending the Homework Hassle* (Rosemond 1990); *How to Help Your Child with Homework: Every Caring Parent's Guide to Encouraging Good Study Habits and Ending the Homework Wars* (Radencich and Schumm 1988)—testifies to the impact of homework on families. Still, families differ on the value they attach to homework. Like my wife and I, many parents resent the intrusion of homework into their families' lives. In these homes, homework is an unwelcome demand on precious time parents would rather spend on family outings or other activities with their children. Other parents welcome homework as a chance to monitor their children's progress at school. A few parents may see homework as a way of keeping their children busy and out of trouble. Some parents, like Gingrich, view homework as a mark of academic rigor necessary for high academic achievement. These parents may insist on more homework from their children's teachers. Some schools also point with pride to the high volume of homework demanded by their teachers to support claims of academic excellence and it's not unusual to occasionally hear parents say something like, "My daughter goes to an excellent school—she has three or four hours of homework every night."

Whatever parents may feel about homework, it is an accepted fact of life in the vast majority of North American homes. The amount of homework families have to contend with, however, will vary from school to school and even from class to class. But, for students who struggle in school, it's probable that they will have *more* homework than their classmates. Based on my interviews with parents whose children struggled in school, it is also likely that the volume of homework combined with the nature of children's academic difficulties (e.g., poor readers, distractible, disorganized, and so on) means that the presence of homework will be especially disruptive and stressful in these families. I'm certain that many of the parents I interviewed would agree with single mother Betty Blake who told me: "The most frustrating thing [for me] right now is homework."

"It's Just Dreadful."

Here's what some of the parents I interviewed had to say about the amount of homework their children had to cope with each night.

"There was always homework . . . ," said Mrs. McIsaac, looking back at her son Robert's first few years in school, "there were hours of homework."

"Peter was bringing home seven, eight, nine pages of [home]work a night," is how John Cooper recalled his son's experience with homework in first grade. "I just thought it was ridiculous for a first grader to do so much work . . . two, two and a half, three hours." Mrs. Cooper added:

> It wasn't difficult work for him to complete. It just took all evening. And sometimes I was getting up in the morning, "Okay, you didn't finish this page, you have to do it before you go to school." And that was something, just driving to school with him doing some homework, finishing a page or something.

"Timmy was bringing home homework like he was in high school," is how Betty Blake recalled the extraordinary amounts of time she and her son, Timmy, devoted to homework assignments. "When he was in second grade I couldn't believe it. . . . We'd get home and we'd be doing homework until ten o'clock at night."

To be fair, a few of the parents I interviewed saw some value in spending so much time doing homework with their children. Mrs. McIsaac had this to say about the benefits of the homework she and her husband did with their son. "He did get a lot out of it. He put a lot into it and he got a lot out of it. It wasn't that bad. . . . He's a very eager boy." Ralph Thorn made a similar comment telling me that all the homework he and his wife did with their son "was starting to pay off right at the end." Mrs. Cooper also tempered her criticism of the volume of homework her son did each night by adding, "this was time we enjoyed."

Still, most parents were not convinced that there was much of a payoff for all the school work their children did at home, nor did they feel that "this was time they enjoyed." Talking about her son's year in ninth grade, Betty Springs observed: "Here's a kid working two, three, and four hours a night and getting just kind of passing grades except in French." I think most of the parents I interviewed would have agreed with Edna Bunker, whose son, Mike, spent "hours and hours and hours on homework. All weekend long, all night long. . . . It's just dreadful," she added. "Just dreadful. It's been really hard."

There was a general feeling among the parents I talked to that their children's learning difficulties were a major factor in the amount of homework their children had to do each night. Several parents indicated that the volume of schoolwork their daughters and sons had to complete at home was a function of work they didn't finish at school. The "hours" of homework Betty Blake's son, Timmy, brought home each night, for example, was mostly work he hadn't completed in school because he spent so much time attending to what was going on around him—a problem that was eventually solved when Timmy's teacher moved his desk to the front of the classroom away from the other children (a suggestion that came from his mother).

Most parents emphasized the effect their children's academic difficulties had on the amount of time it took to complete their homework. Talking about the time he and his wife spent working with their son's homework, Ralph Thorn recalled: "It would take us two, three hours, four hours every night trying, the two of us, *trying to get through fifteen, twenty minutes worth of homework.*" Here's how Mr. Thorn described homework sessions with his son, Al:

> In a household where there are other outside noises going on and everything, the slightest little disruption, I mean, it's not that something was disrupting, Al would focus on what was going on, it was just that Al was focusing on everything that was going on . . . it was a pretty difficult task, for both of us.

The attention deficit disorder that underlay their son's academic struggles at school was, presumably, the reason it took "three or four hours every night" to get through "fifteen, twenty minutes worth of homework."

Edna Bunker, on the other hand, blamed her son, Mike's, "perfectionism" for the excessive amount of time she felt he devoted to his homework. Mrs. Bunker offered the following example of how her son's desire for everything to be perfect made things so difficult for both of them.

> For example, this year he had to do something for language arts. And he was like 98 percent finished in rough. And because he is a perfectionist, it wasn't finished enough for him. And so he was ready to throw the whole thing away and not even– and, like, I said, "Mike, just do the good copy, just hand it in as it is, so the teacher will think you don't have an ending but at least you will get some marks." But he was ready to dump the whole thing because he gets so frustrated. Because it's not the way he wants it. He spends hours and hours and hours on homework. All weekend long, all night long. . . . Everything is such a slow process. Like if he's doing a title page it's taking him all day to do it because it is not the way he wants it to be or . . . you know. It's just really frustrating.

Overall, the parents I interviewed emphasized that homework ate up huge chunks of time both for their children and for them as they endeavored to offer the support their children needed to complete the work they brought home from school each night. I discuss different ways parents were involved in their children's homework in the following section.

"I Couldn't Leave Her on Her Own."

In the homes of many of our friends there is a quiet place for their children to do homework away from the noise and distractions of family activities. In these homes homework is generally a solitary activity undertaken by children without much intervention by their parents. Certainly children may seek the help of parents or siblings with the spelling of a word, a difficult math problem, or confusing directions. Many parents also have to remind (read: nag) their children to do their homework, but, by and large, homework doesn't place too many demands on parents beyond the occasional school project that turns many homes upside down.

For the families of struggling students I talked to, however, homework was usually a collaborative activity involving parents and children. There were differences in the nature of support children required and the kind of support their parents were able to provide but, in general, if homework made significant demands on students who struggled in school it made similar demands on their parents. Mrs. Dumay, for example, bemoaned the fact that her daughter, Georgina, wasn't able to do her homework independently because, in her opinion, Georgina lacked "confidence."

> Oh, [homework] was a problem. I had to sit right there with her. I couldn't leave her on her own . . . 'cause she didn't work independently. She always wanted you there, to do, to help her [but] not to actually do it. I'd like have to read the directions two or three times. Say, "this is what they want you to do." She found the independent work hard and had a hard time doing it. I had to be right there. Sitting right there with her, you know. I don't think that was too much of a problem, but I didn't want her to get the idea that I was doing it for her. I didn't want her to get that idea. And I think that sometimes that's what she wanted. "Well, Mom, what does that mean? Is that the answer? Is that the answer?" I'd say, "Read it. Let's read it together and then you tell me what you think." Things like that. I think that she kind of got the idea that I was doing the work for her. She wanted me to. If I'm sitting there she'd ask me right then: "What's that?" "Is that right?" "Do you think?" And she had another problem with wondering if it's right and all. If it wasn't right, "Mom is that right?" "Is that right?" "Should I put that down?" Stuff like that. "I don't know where that goes." I don't understand that. She had no confidence.

Georgina needed this kind of constant support from her mother while she did homework when she was in first and second grade, but even parents of older children told me that their daughters and sons often insisted that someone at least sit with them while they did their homework. Edna Bunker spoke of her thirteen-year-old son, Mike's, need for her to "be there" while he did his homework and her frustrations with demands on her time that "go on and on."

> Mike wants someone to sit one-on-one with him [while he does his homework]. And so I'll do that for awhile, but, see, I also get frustrated too because it goes on and on and on. It's not like he can just sit there and get the stuff done quickly. It goes on and on. He gets distracted and it's just going on for so long and so it's frustrating.

If all the parents didn't feel that they needed to sit with their children all the time they were doing homework, most talked about the time they had to spend monitoring children's homework and helping them to organize their work. Each day Mrs. Bunker, for example, met Mike at the door with a big "stop" sign which was her humorous way of asking her son to stop and think: "Do you know what homework you have tonight?" "Do you have what you need to complete your homework?" and so on. As she put it, "He comes home for lunch and he comes home at the end of the day and you're monitoring."

Many parents told me that "nagging" was the principal means they used to make sure their children's homework was completed. "Every day I go in," Elma Kinkead said, "and ask [her teenage daughter] Andrea, 'Have you done your homework?' 'What are you doing?' 'What kind of marks are you getting?' 'Why don't you leave me alone?' 'Of course, I've done my homework,' she'll tell me. 'No, don't tell me you've done your homework.'" Mrs. Riggs told a similar story. "I'm badgering my son every night for his homework," she said. "You know, he loves the computer so he's on the computer. 'Roger, come on, let's do *our* homework.' 'Okay, well wait a minute,' he'll say." I imagine Edna Bunker spoke for many parents when she told me, "It's always, 'Do you have it done?' All day long. If you would hear us. That's all we're saying. Hurry up and get it done. Hurry up so that we can do something else."

Other parents talked about using encouragement to get their children to do their homework, but whether encouragement or nagging, the parents I talked with expended a lot of time and emotional energy getting their children to complete the school work they brought home each evening. Parents generally felt that without frequent reminders and careful monitoring their children would have difficulty even beginning to do their homework. "Mike is so disorganized," Mrs. Bunker told me. Mike was among many children whose parents told me frequently failed to write down assignments or left assignments or materials needed to compete homework assignments at school. Catherine Connor's description of her son, Max, was fairly typical: "Typically, Max does not bring home the textbook that's got the homework he needs. He always forgets that, he forgets the assignments."

There were a range of strategies the parents I interviewed used to keep track of their children's homework. If children left needed materials at school, for example, some parents, like Edna Bunker, would drive them back to school to collect whatever they needed to complete their homework. For other parents, Mr. and Mrs. Moore, for example, this was something they only threatened to do. Speaking of the difficulty of monitoring Archie's homework, Mrs. Moore told me, "If he doesn't write it down, and he doesn't do it, I have no way of checking it—unless I get him in the car and take him back out there every day." When I asked her if she had ever taken him back to school she said, "No, I've threatened to," to which her husband added, "I don't think you've ever taken him back."

What helped Catherine Conner keep track of her son, Max's, homework was regular communication from Max's teacher and the willingness of the school to let her and her husband borrow a set of textbooks (not all schools would even have an extra set to lend). Mrs. Conner and her husband found that they were able to help Max keep up with his homework "if we can find out from his teacher what assignments are coming up—and they are very good about it—and they give us an extra set of textbooks to keep at home." But keeping track of Max's homework still demanded lots of their time.

Homework books were, perhaps, the most common strategy teachers and parents used to try to help children keep track of their homework. Each day teachers checked to see if students recorded all their assignments in their homework books, which parents signed to indicate that they had indeed checked the homework books. A few parents told me that they found homework books a useful way to monitor their children's homework. Other parents indicated that, since the success of homework books depended on children's initiative and follow-through, this strategy was doomed from the start. One mom told me, "we have never really done a successful job keeping track of our son's homework. We always say we are going to do a homework tracking between us and the teacher that either says 'no homework' or this is what's due. But those slips typically never make it home and we are always battling to make sure that we get that." Archie Moore's teacher told his parents that she would agree to the use of a homework book only on the condition that it was initiated by Archie. "The thing is," Archie's father told me, "sometimes he does forget his work. What's really bad is you know how he's supposed to have an assignment book. . . . That is a no go. I mean, and I've asked his teacher and she says, 'Well, if Archie will take it upon himself to bring it up to me, I will sign it and fill it out.'" Apparently, this never happens. Maybe Archie felt like Steve Thibault, who rejected homework books because he felt that he was too old for them. Archie and Steve may have also resisted homework books because, like my daughter, they felt that homework books were a badge of dishonor, a kind of "Scarlet S" that marked them as "stupid." In any case, parents' ability to monitor their children's homework depended on the compliance of their sons and daughters. "I'm lost," Mrs. Moore said, "because his homework may be posted on the board, it may be by their lockers, whatever, but if he doesn't write it down, and he doesn't do it, I have no way of checking it unless I get him in the car and take him back out there every day." Arguably, strategies that rely on the organizational skills of children whose school struggles are related to poor organization in the first place have little chance of succeeding.

I suspect that all the parents I interviewed would agree with Diane Riggs about the importance of helping their children with homework.

> I have to make sure that Roger's got his homework done. If I don't, then he gets behind and the teacher gets cross with him and, you

know, he starts feeling badly about himself. If he can keep up and at least have his homework done, then he's all right. It's when he gets behind he gets panicky and starts feeling badly about himself.

The cost of letting homework slide is high, as Mrs. Riggs suggests. The price of getting children to complete their homework—monitoring, encouraging, nagging, driving back to school to retrieve materials, and arguing—is also high and, for some of the parents I interviewed, the aggravation and tension over homework may have outweighed any benefits of getting it done. "It's not worth it," as one parent told me. This may account for Mr. and Mrs. Moore's willingness to accept their son's frequent assertion that "I don't have any homework." I suspect they knew differently, but to accept his claim was much easier that fighting over homework. David Thibault put it well.

> You fear that if your kid doesn't do well in school then their life is going to be hell and they're going to ruin their life. And what they have to do is take school seriously and always do better at it. But in trying to push your kid to do better at school, and constantly insisting that there is always more homework to do—and there is always more effort to put into this stuff—you end up, I think, often ruining the relationship that you have with your kid. When school is over, you still want to have a relationship where you get enjoyment and satisfaction and you want to have a good relationship with your children and the school gets in the way because you're constantly nagging that you have to do better in school, you have to do more homework, you have to put more effort in.

I've often heard teachers complain that parents who fail to monitor their children's homework "don't really care" about their children's education. I doubt that these teachers have any idea of the demands homework often make on the parents of children for whom school is a struggle. Nor do I imagine that many teachers understand that, for parents like the Moores and the Thibaults, deliberately avoiding endless struggles over homework with their children is an expression of caring. In the eyes of these parents, damaging long- and short-term relationships with their children is just too high price to pay for meeting the demands of the school.

"Work with Her at Home."

Most of the parents I interviewed indicated that they felt it was necessary to supervise their children's homework on a regular basis. Many said that they also had to provide lots of support and encouragement to help their children do their homework—even sitting by their children's side as they did their homework as in the cases of Mrs. Bunker and Mrs. Dumay. However necessary monitoring, supervision, nagging, and encouragement were to get students to complete their homework, these general strategies were rarely sufficient in the case of parents whose children struggled in school. When Tiffany Scott's teacher informed her mother that Tiffany "wasn't up to her level," Mrs. Scott asked Tiffany's teacher what she should do. The teacher's response was that she "work with her [Tiffany] at home." Many parents I interviewed took up the challenge to "work with" their children at home. Parents differed, however, in the nature of the assistance they offered their children as well as their ability to provide explicit support and direction for their children's homework. Diane Riggs, for example, spoke of the wide range of ways she supported her son Roger's school work.

> Every night there's always something. Either grammar—his math he's very good at so I don't have to worry about that, unless it comes out with problems, word problems, then I have to go through and read it for him. I'm sitting right down here and I'm saying, "Well, what do you have to do?" And if it's grammar I have to read through it and it's quite often fill in the blanks or it might be a book report or something like that and I have to help him with his spelling, trying to figure out what he wants to say. So I'm doing a lot of the work, yes.

Many parents found that they "did a lot of the work" and, in general, they did whatever they thought was necessary to help their sons and daughters complete their homework assignments satisfactorily. Edna Bunker went so far as to gather resources for her son's assignments, taking advantage of the fact that she didn't work outside the home. She spoke of the range of supports she provided for her son's homework and how time-consuming this was for her:

> I'm spending all my time doing for him, all my time. I go to the library. . . . Like I'll say to him, "What are you studying about in geography? Tell me what you are studying about." [Then] I will go to the library and try and find books on it so he's got extra resources.

This level of support was extraordinary among the parents I interviewed. More typical was Tanya Wallace, who supported her daughter by helping her to edit and/or revise her written work. Mrs. Wallace talked both about helping her daughter with her writing and the demands this placed on her and her husband.

> We used to help Catherine a lot with her, editing her writing because of her spelling. But the oral—her understanding and the language was fabulous. But when it came to writing it—that's when things fell apart. . . . So in seventh and eighth grade we would edit for her. We tried everything. But then rewriting took so long. . . . Ninth grade came and we said, well she's got to learn to do this on her own because

we're not. . . . I work full time [and] my husband works full time. [So] we got a computer.

Mr. and Mrs. Wallace hoped that a word processor with a spelling and grammar checker would give Catherine the support she needed and relieve them of the burden of always having to edit Catherine's writing.

Mr. and Mrs. Moore talked about using "tricks" to help Archie complete his homework.

> Sometimes I would have to, if I knew he was very tired, I'd have to find an alternative way to do it. Like sometimes maybe I trick him and say he had twenty math questions to do. I'd have him write out the first four, and I'd do them, and he would correct me. . . . I'd do them, but he was watching over me doing them. Just to add some variety. Then he'd get a boost from that, so then he'd do the next one. Just to try and alternate things. Sometimes we'd do tricks like that to make it less stressful. He would actually be doing the math but I would be doing the writing.

In much the same way, the Moores tried to get Archie to read "chapter books" by reading alternate pages for him. "He hates reading, he won't read chapter books. I've tried I read a page, he reads a page," Mrs. Moore told me.

Supporting children's reading was another way many of the parents I talked to helped their children with their homework. Carol Dumay talked about how she tried to promote Georgina's reading development through the use of general encouragement and specific teaching strategies (e.g., "Go back and read it again.").

> Instead of saying, "Oh, I think that's great," or "Wow!" You say to her, "That's good." That's what I do all the time, I do that still now. "You read that. That's good." "That sounded so nice." Because before she read like "The—cow—was," you know, she paused after every word and I told her just to pause at the period. Always, just pause at the period. Whereas I think she was so anxious to get it right, that she would try to go fast and then she was still stumbling on the word. I knew [that] she knew. And I said, "Go back and read it again. Do it over."

Mrs. Dumay also supported Georgina's reading development by

> letting her read to me [and] I read to her constantly. My husband would read to her. We'd go to the library, let her pick the books. I gave her money to buy books. I said, "Would you like to buy your book?" Well before that, "No, I don't want to buy a book." But now she wants to buy a book. Like, if I give her money, "Can I buy this book? That book?" And I say, "Fine." So she's changed a lot with that. It seemed that books were a no-no. She didn't want to look at that. But now it's like, "I got to have a book." But we were helping her with just reading and showing her.

Mrs. Dumay supported her daughter's reading development, in part, by drawing on strategies (e.g., "Go back. . . .") she had learned from the staff at a special reading program at the local university.

I imagine that Carol Dumay saw her work in support of her daughter's reading development as augmenting the efforts of Georgina's teachers and the staff at the university reading clinic. Celine Street, on the other hand, saw her efforts to "teach" her son to read as a means of overcoming what she believed were the shortcomings of her son's teacher(s). When Dennis was in third grade she

> found that Dennis can really focus on a lot of things if you know how to do it right. And he requires, like I said, participation. If I read to him, he would read to me. We would read a book together. It started with, we still have them, and they're still one of his favorites. They're the Disney baby characters. You get a story and you read some words and there's a character. The character will tell you what that word is. So I would read and he would tell me what the character was. Or I would read and then we would switch it around. He would read and I would do the character. Now he is reading books that are at the higher level than a lot of children his age. He doesn't want to read the baby books [anymore].

Each and every parent I interviewed was anxious to do everything in their power to help their children with their school work. There was, however, a frequently expressed concern about the tension between *helping* children do their school work and *doing* it for them. "The temptation is to want to do too much. You want to help too much," Mrs. Wallace told me. Mrs. Scott put it this way: "I didn't want my daughter to get the idea that I was doing it for her." A troubling story told to me by Martin and Betty Springs made it clear how fine the line between *helping* and *doing* can be, at least from the perspective of teachers.

> Sam had about two pages of notes [for his assignment on the Venus's-flytrap]. So I said to him, "Put it into a draft. Give me a draft," 'cause he asked if I would help him. So I said yeah, but come to me with a draft first. So he did that. He had the rough notes and he had this draft. And I read it and it was . . . he had some good information that was really scattered and I said to him, "You have a lot of really good information here, but it's kind of scattered and I think what I can do is help you to organize it." He said, "That's what I want you to do." So I said, "Read the first sentence." He read the whole thing to me out loud and he automatically began making corrections. For him, if he reads it orally, that's how he is able to punctuate. He does all those kinds of things. So I said all right, let's look at what you are saying here and we'll look at that other stuff later, after. So I said, "Read the first sentence out loud to me." And he read it out loud. "What's it about?"

He said, "Well, it describes the plant." So I said, "Put a little [number] one beside that." So he did that. I said, "Read through the rest of it and find all the sentences that talk about what this plant looks like." So he did that. Just did it. I said, "Second sentence. What's that about?" "Well where you'd find it, the habitat." I said, "All right, do the same thing. Put a [number] two." He did that. He says, "Oh. I get it. I'll do that." So he took it away, did all that reorganization and brought it back, but he was having a fit cause it has to be four pages, not two and he only had two. It had to be four. I said, "All right, why did you pick a Venus's-flytrap?" Like I said, "Where did that come from?" He said, "Oh, well I saw it in horror movies . . . I saw it in *Little Shop of Horrors* and it was really big and it ate people and everything else." I said, "Well put that in." So he put it in. And I said, "Now, your sister had a little Venus's-flytrap." She had to have it. Bought it at a nursery. And they're like about this big and it takes about six weeks for them to do anything. And I said, "How is this Venus's-flytrap, the real one, different than the one you saw in the *Little Shop of Horrors*?" Oh he had all sorts of details. I said, "Put that in." So he put all that stuff in. He was describing it and he talked about the mechanism where it closes, as the insects fly by they trigger a mechanism that triggers the closing. And I said, "What around here does that remind you of?" He said, "I don't know." I said, "When I put the dogs out at night in the back yard, what happens?" He said, "Oh, the light goes on." He said, "It's the movement that triggers that light to go on." I said, "Yeah. It's the same, isn't it?" I said, "It sounds like it would be the same." "I'll put that in," he said. He put all those things in. He got it up to the four pages. He typed it. I said, "You go through and you highlight the words you think are misspelled." Out of that four pages he had six spelling mistakes. He was able to recognize all of them. And he corrected them. Then he went through and he read it to me and said, "I used the word 'important' too many times." I said, "Yeah, you have." I said, "Let's get the thesaurus out." He didn't know what a thesaurus was. So, it was like he discovered a gold mine. . . . That took place over about three evenings. And of the three evenings, he worked a couple of hours, he spent out of maybe two or three hours work, fifteen minutes with me. And he took it away and he did what he needed to do. So when it was all done, I said, "Read it back to me," and he did and he looked at me and he said, "It's too good, Mom." I said, "What do you mean?" He said, "They're going to think it's not mine. It's too good." I said, "Mike, that's not a problem. You've got your notes here and you've got the rough draft." His father said, "Yeah, you have to hand it all in together." I said, "It's not a problem."

As it turned out, Mike's teacher did conclude that his paper was "too good."

So he put it all together and he said, "She checked the notes. She saw the rough draft." So she took it away. He didn't get it back, didn't get it back, didn't get it back. And about three weeks later I said to him,

"Have you got that paper back yet?" And he said, "She said that there was a problem with it and she wanted to read it again and check it out." I said, "Oh, all right." So he came back a couple of days later and said to me, "I got zero." And I said, "Why?" He said, "Because she said it's too good to be mine."

Betty Springs is a teacher with a Masters degree and a background in special education. Her professional background gave her access to strategies that were particularly useful for helping her high school-aged son revise his assignment on Venus's-flytraps. Many teachers are on the alert, however, for students who receive "too much" help from their parents and, in this case, because Sam's work contradicted the teacher's expectations about his ability, the teacher concluded that Sam's work was not his own. To my way of thinking this is grossly unfair. The nature of Mrs. Springs' support for Sam's assignment was, in my opinion, just right even if it was a kind of support few parents— most of whom are not teachers—could have provided. Ideally, teachers should be delighted when struggling students do excellent work and not suspicious that excellence probably means cheating. Still, cheating does occur and many teachers will always feel a need to consider work completed out of the classroom in terms of their overall assessment of students' ability. Determining what counts as help and what constitutes too much help isn't easy for teachers even if I would prefer that, wherever possible, teachers give students the benefit of the doubt.

This episode demonstrates the fine line between *helping* and *doing* that parents of students who struggle in school may have to negotiate. Clearly, one person's *helping* may be another person's *doing* and, if the teacher concludes that parents' help has crossed the line to *doing*, the child/student may be in peril. This possibility is a further complication for parents who want to help their children with their schoolwork.

"This Is Mom's Homework."

When I interviewed Mrs. Lau, a Chinese woman who had emigrated from Taiwan with her husband, her daughter, Bonnie, was enrolled in a full-time class for children with "language disabilities." (Although Bonnie spoke Mandarin at home with her parents school officials attributed her difficulty acquiring spoken English to a language disability and placed her in a special class.) Mrs. Lau told me that she typically spent one and a half to two hours each night doing homework with Bonnie. Although Bonnie sometimes had to write in her journal for homework, the bulk of the schoolwork Mrs. Lau did with her daughter was what Mrs. Lau called "mom's homework." In general, Mrs. Lau sought to bring her daughter's school work up to grade level using an age-graded "super workbook" (full of drills and exercises in math, reading, writing, and spelling) which was used by other parents in the Chinese community and she was able to purchase from a "teachers' store" in the mall. Mrs. Lau offered the following example of "mom's homework":

> In their school they are only teaching them two-digit addition and subtraction. Only this. But now my daughter can do multiplication. I taught her. I do everything in the nighttime. I don't know what they're teaching there [in Bonnie's *special* school]. I don't know. I have to work by myself. I don't know what's right or wrong.

"Mom's homework" differed from the usual homework because it was not assigned by teachers. This was more like tutoring in the sense that it was aimed at the general strengthening of children's academic abilities rather than support for specific school assignments. Mrs. Lau taught her daughter math skills she felt that the school should have been teaching her.

> She's only doing second grade now and she has a problem doing this book. Very, very worrisome. She's third grade but she has a problem doing third grade homework. She's doing very, very slowly. Christmas now and she's only done 100 pages [of the super workbook] and she doesn't want to continue. She says stop, so we stop the work. So she's doing very, very, very slowly.

Like Celine Street, who took it upon herself to teach her son to read when he didn't learn to read at school, and Betty Blake, who asked her son's teacher to assign him extra math work so that "I could work with him at home," Mrs. Lau took on the role of her daughter's tutor in an effort to help her "catch up" academically. This recalls my own efforts to teach my daughter to read when she was in second grade (see Chapter 1).

Alice Mandel took advantage of the knowledge she had acquired during her graduate training in education to help her daughter, Ruth, learn some of the skills she needed to overcome her "learning disability." Like many other parents, Mr. and Mrs. Mandel helped Ruth with proofreading and editing her written assignments, but Mrs. Mandel also wanted to help Ruth "learn how to learn." For example:

> Like before exams though, I spent hours and hours with her. You know . . . show her how to study, how to make herself ask questions. When I asked her questions, she's to write them out. And then we review them. Help her remember things. Give her mnemonics, that kind of thing. Before exams we do spend an awful lot of time with her.

Teaching Ruth how to study was just one of a number of learning strategies Alice Mandel taught her daughter.

Of course, few parents I interviewed had the training and experience to teach their children study skills as Alice Mandel did nor did they have the time or inclination to do the kind of "mom's homework" undertaken nightly by Mrs. Lau. Most were busy enough just helping their children complete the homework assignments sent home by teachers.

A few of the parents I interviewed were able to supplement their own efforts to help their children with their homework with private tutoring. Typically, private tutoring went beyond daily homework assignments by focusing on the strengthening of children's reading and writing skills. Carol Dumay was interested in taking her daughter to a Sylvan Learning Center, a commercial tutoring program, which would "go back to where the problem starts." Her husband, however, vetoed this option as "too expensive" (Mrs. Dumay told me that it would have cost $100 just to have her daughter tested). Many of the parents I interviewed were able to arrange some kind of private tutoring, however. The McIsaacs and the Riggs, for example, were able to take their children to Sylvan for extra help even if, as in the case of Diane Riggs who took both her children to Sylvan "twice a week at $40 an hour," this may have imposed a bit of a financial hardship in the short term. Michelle Phills, who could not have afforded such expensive tutoring, found a university-sponsored reading clinic that offered her daughter tutoring on a weekly basis.

In the end, homework was a major factor in how the parents I interviewed lived their lives and there is no reason to believe that the time tension, frustration, and, in some cases, the expense of private tutoring improved the quality of their lives. In fact, the evidence presented here suggests quite the opposite. Homework was, no doubt, part of the reason Mrs. Moore told me that "the month of August, when it comes, I get depressed." When their children struggle in school, the coming of August means school will be starting soon and homework will again become an unwelcome focus in their lives. Mrs. Reeves may have said it best: "Homework is a hassle. Just about every day it's a hassle." I'm certain that no teacher wishes to disrupt students' families through homework, so teachers who take seriously the concerns of these parents may have to rethink their homework policies. This is something I take up in more detail in the final chapter of this book but, for now, I acknowledge that the development of fair and flexible homework policies for all students will not be easy and, ultimately, will require some level of collaboration between teachers, parents, and, most importantly, students.

Homework was a major source of tension in the homes of the families I interviewed which affected the relationships of parents with their children, with each other, and with siblings. The effects of school troubles on family relationships is the topic of the next chapter.

Chapter Five

School Troubles
and Family Tensions

School affected my relationship with Robert. . . . I think if I had kept him in school it would have caused a barrier between us. There was always homework. There were hours of homework. In the evening sitting at the kitchen table just doing it over and over and over again. So it was quite stressful. It did create quite a stress. So when we took him out of school [for homeschooling], it removed the third party. It was just Robert and I. For the first few weeks, it was difficult. . . . There was like the pressure off all the time. Now it's very easygoing. You don't really have to make him do the stuff . . . having him out it's easier. I think it could have only gotten worse.

—Interview with
Sheila McIsaac

Families are made up of individuals: mothers, fathers, sons, daughters, grandmothers, grandfathers, aunts, uncles, cousins. It would be a mistake, however, to think of a family as *merely* a collection of individuals. Families are fluid, complex, organic *systems* in which each family member, each part of the system, affects and is affected by every part of the system (Green 1995; Turnbull and Turnbull 1986). When a child is born, for example, the number of people living in the family system is increased by one, but the family is not merely larger. The relationships between and among family members are transformed by the addition of the new person. First children demand that spouses expand their relationship beyond husband and wife to include the roles of mother and father. Similarly, the birth of a sibling dictates that an "only child" revise her or his standing in the family to accommodate the new (and not always welcome) role of brother or sister. Any change in the mix at any time in the life cycle of a family will transform the family organism, demanding that family members adjust to the change—individually and collectively. Families also have to accommodate changes in lives of individual family members. Children starting school, the emergence of adolescence and adulthood, illness, the loss of a job, divorce, or the death of a family member are among the possible influences on the life of a family. Of course, families do not always adapt to change successfully, but the failure to adjust to changes in the family system can be expected to have negative consequences on the lives of individual family members.

Although change is never easy, most families manage to cope with life's exigencies. How families cope with their circumstances is, however, a function of the resources they can draw upon within the family and the communities of which they are a part (neighborhood, church, civic organizations, and so on). The availability of financial and community resources, the presence of extended family, spiritual beliefs, and friends and neighbors are among the factors that can affect how well families adapt to change both within and outside the family (Turnbull and Turnbull, 1986). But one thing is certain: there will be change and families will have to adjust.

The demand on families that is of particular interest here is the presence of a child for whom school is a struggle and, among the families I interviewed, a son or daughter who struggled in school always had a significant effect on the roles and relationships of family members.

"There's Always Tension in This House."

When Edna Bunker told me, "There's a lot of tension. There's always tension in this house," she recalled my own experience with our daughter, Anne's, struggles in school. The tension over schooling in our house was palpable (see Chapter 1). Many of the parents I spoke to also referred to a general tension in their households which they attributed to their children's struggles in school. Janet Moore, for example, was explicit about the relationship between the tension in their house and school trouble: "I don't look forward to school starting because of the fighting and all that." Summers were good in the Moore household—

calm and peaceful, Mrs. Moore believed, *because* she and the rest of her family didn't have to cope with homework and other hassles related to schooling.

Of course, all families have to cope with school. Last-minute attention to school assignments, heavy homework nights, school concerts, teacher conferences, and exams all intrude on the lives of families with school children, as Amy Thibault, the mother of four children, observed:

> Around this house we always have to be concerned with school deadlines. Keeping track of exam periods and deadlines so we don't go away for weekends or let the kids take extended overnights which might interfere with their school work. Like holidays, social events, you always have to be aware of where that fits with regard to school scheduling. Because it can easily break down. Deciding that you are going to go skiing for the weekend can lead to a bit of a breakdown because the family chores haven't been done and also this carryover, people fighting by Wednesday because the laundry wasn't done and somebody hasn't done their homework. It doesn't take much to muck up the whole schedule of homework, deadlines, major assignments. Like it all has to be kind of sandwiched in. I think we are relatively organized, but not getting to a library or not picking up something needed for schoolwork really tips it all upside-down very fast.

In the Thibault family, like many other families, the ordinary demands of schooling routinely created tensions, but coping with the anxieties and the material demands of meeting the needs of children who struggle in school can be especially difficult. Focusing on just one consequence of living with school trouble, Mrs. Wallace confided that, "There's been a lot of anxiety because of a child going through a testing procedure. It's anxiety-provoking for the whole family." She added that meeting the financial demands of independent testing and seeking remedial assistance added to her family's anxieties.

Parents of children who struggle in school have to cope not only with stress created by the immediate demands of school trouble, they also have to deal with the possibility of future tensions, as the following comment by Amy Thibault suggests.

> We are quite worried that if Steve fails one of his courses—I'm thinking of a course that he's just barely passing right now—if he fails that course now that means the certain prospect of summer school. And that means, of course, lots and lots of aggravation. . . . First of all, Steve is going to fight like hell against it and that's just going to be something else to fight about and there'll be the tensions around that and then there are the concerns about how's he going to get there. His sister is going to take a math course this summer, so she could drive him. But it is far enough away that he couldn't get back on his own. Since her course goes 9:00 to 3:00 and his will go 9:00 to 12:00, what

is he going to do from 12:00 to 3:00? This creates a situation where he is sitting around for three hours a day and, not just sitting around, hanging around in Newtown for three hours a day and there's lots of trouble to be gotten into.

As Mrs. Thibault makes clear, school troubles not only disrupt the lives of families lives in the present, but they also create worry over the possibility of future tensions and aggravation.

For most of the families I talked to, school trouble was just one more demand in their already overburdened lives. Edna Bunker's return to school to pursue a degree in social work created tension by requiring other family members to contribute more to running the household. This was stressful enough, but the additional demands imposed by her son's struggles in school (homework, frequent phone calls to teachers, and so on) pushed her family nearly to the breaking point. Family counseling helped to relieve some of the tension. However, when I interviewed Mrs. Bunker, she had completed her degree but was delaying her entry into the job so that she could provide the support she believed her son needed to cope with school. This decision created its own stress for Edna Bunker and her family.

Single mothers like Molly Reeves and Betty Blake also spoke of trying to cope with homework, domestic chores, and full-time commitments outside the home. Molly Reeves said that most nights, because her sons required so much support from her for their schoolwork, she was unable to wash dishes, clean house, or do laundry until after 10:00 when she was already exhausted. Betty Blake didn't get home until after 6:00 and many nights she had to rush dinner so that there would be enough time for homework. School trouble was stressful for all the families I interviewed, but probably nowhere was the stress greater than in single-parent households, an issue I'll say more about in the next chapter.

Even without the complications of housework, paid employment, and homework, the mere presence of a child who was unhappy in school was stressful enough for these parents. Mrs. Phills explained: "There's continuous upheaval in this house because there is a kid that's very upset because she can't pursue her interest. She's highly motivated and wants to do things, but can't get access to it because of her problems with school." Jamie Frick would have agreed. Her daughter's frustrations with school were a constant source of conflict and tension in their house.

Some parents attempted to reduce the tension in their houses by trying to "put things into perspective." Mr. and Mrs. Springs' aspirations for their son to go to college and achieve vocational and financial success, for example, were threatened by his struggles in school.

The Springs attempted to cope with their fears over Sam's future by focusing on Sam's happiness which, they tried to convince themselves,
wasn't necessarily linked to financial and academic success. This is how
Martin Springs put it: "As long as you're happy. You can have an old
clunker. You can have a rented house. You can be living somewhere in
a trailer if you want or bunking somewhere, as long as you're happy."
When I asked if he found it difficult to accept his own advice, Mr. Springs
conceded that it was.

Our society places considerable stock in schooling. Most Americans
believe that school is the great equalizer: With hard work and a good
education a child can grow up to be whatever he or she wants (recalling the aphorism, "anyone can grow up to be president"). Alternatively,
most parents probably believe that poor performance in school will diminish their children's chances of success and happiness. Mr. Springs
desire to separate his son's success in school from his long-term happiness flies in the face of a strong cultural belief that schooling is crucial
to any child or adult's life chances. In this cultural context, school failure is bound to be stressful.

Another strategy some parents used to try to reduce school-related
stress in their households was to *simply refuse* to accept the demands of
schooling. Recall from the previous chapter David Thibault's observation about the tension between insisting that his son Steve put forth the
effort to do well in school and his desire to maintain a satisfying relationship with Steve after he graduates from high school. "When school
is over, you still want to have a relationship where you get enjoyment
and satisfaction and you want to have a good relationship with your
children," is how he put it. But Mr. Thibault made it clear how difficult
it was to reduce the tensions over schooling in his family. Talking about
what has to happen for schoolwork not be a source of tension in their
house on any given evening, he said:

> For the thing to work, Steve has to come home and say, "I think I am
> going to do some more schoolwork today," and it has to be on one of
> the days when I say, "I wish Steve would really put his attention into
> his schoolwork," and a day when [Steve's mother] Amy says, "You
> know, I really think that it's in Steve's best interest to work at school."
> Then we are harmonious and everything is great. Or, when he would
> come home and say, "I've had enough," and I say, "Get off the kid's
> back," and [his mother] says, "Let him have some fun," then it's okay.
> But the likelihood of that happening is very remote. He comes home
> and needs a break, I say, "Give the kid a break, let's not bug him about
> school" and it happens to be a day when his mother thinks schooling
> is very important and so she gets on his case. Or it could be the op-
> posite. For there not to be tension and disagreement on a day-to-day
> basis as to how important school is and whether the next three hours
> have to be given over to yet more homework, yet more attention paid

to school—the likelihood of that happening is just real remote. So there's always [tension]. If it's not between Steve and me, it's me and Amy, or between Amy and Steve. I mean there's always the possibility for people to be thinking differently about how important school is on any given day.

When I asked Mr. and Mrs. Moore how their lives would be different if their son, Archie, didn't struggle in school they said, "There would be less arguing." But, of course, Archie wasn't doing better in school and the arguing continued. Other parents I interviewed did manage to find relief from the stress of school troubles when their children began to do better in school. The McIsaacs, for example, found their lives "very easygoing" once they took their son out of school in favor of homeschooling.

Other parents I interviewed who decided either to homeschool their children or enroll their sons or daughters in schools (public and private) that were more congenial to their needs also talked about a reduced level of stress. Over a year after I interviewed Jamie Frick, she called to tell me that her relationship with her daughter Debbie had improved dramatically since Debbie had enrolled in an alternative public high school. I've had a similar experience in my family. We still have the occasional fight over homework assignments or poor test results, but the constant, and sometimes debilitating, tension over schooling disappeared after we enrolled Anne in an alternative private school.

Overall, the parents I interviewed made it clear that, directly or indirectly, their children's struggles in school were a frequent and palpable source of stress in their lives which, at the very least, exacerbated existing tensions in their households. In the rest of this chapter, I'll discuss parents' perceptions of how school troubles affected specific relationships between and among family members.

"I Just Dislike Her Attitude."

Single mom Maria Scott offered the following example of the kind of interactions that she and Tiffany, her only child, had when they worked together on Tiffany's schoolwork.

> So I'll say to Tiffany, "OK let's read. I'll read one page and you read a page." So I'd read a page and she'd listen to me read and then, when it's time for her to read, she'd get frustrated when she got stuck on a word. I don't know if it was because when I read I was going through with it and she wanted to go through the words exactly the same way or if she wanted to get through the story just as quickly as I got through it with that first page. And she just sat there and got so upset. And sometimes she would make me upset and I would say, "Tiffany,

you know this word. Start with the first letter and sound it out." And she'd get upset so we're both sitting there trying to figure out this word. And sometimes I would even say, "Oh, just forget it!" Because, see, I didn't know what to do. I'd get so frustrated. If she sits there and gets mad at me because I won't tell her this word and I'm trying to help her sound the word out . . . I would yell and say, "Well just go! Just leave me alone!" And she'd get upset and started to cry and all that.

In the end, Ms. Scott believed that doing homework with Tiffany did neither of them much good: "It damaged my daughter as well as our relationship," she said. "Whenever we did homework we were fussing and fighting and getting frustrated with each other."

Like every parent I interviewed, Maria Scott believed that school was critical to her daughter's future. But even more important to Ms. Scott was her relationship with her daughter, Tiffany, whom, she confided, was "all she has." This relationship was imperiled, in Ms. Scott's opinion, by "fussing and fighting and getting frustrated" over Tiffany's schoolwork. Maria desperately wanted to enjoy the time she spent with her daughter, but the exigencies of schooling demanded that Ms. Scott focus their time together on teaching Tiffany things her daughter didn't want to learn and do schoolwork she didn't want to do, hence the "fussing and fighting."

Molly Reeves described similar tensions when she tried to help her son read a passage containing his weekly spelling words.

It was one day last week. It was some of his spelling words: fast, faster; tall, taller. Just add -er, you know. And there was a little story he had to read that had some of his spelling words. And *fast,* he got it, but every time we got to *faster,* he didn't get it. And there was no difference, you know, except the ending. We just kept arguing over it. And finally I said, "All right, just let it go, forget it. Go on." And he went into his room.

Almost every parent I talked to told me that their efforts to help their sons and daughters with their schoolwork were fraught with the same sort of tensions and frustrations described by Maria Scott and Molly Reeves. This isn't so unusual by itself. I imagine that all parents, like Maria Scott and Molly Reeves, take on the role of their children's teacher from time to time, perhaps helping their children with a difficult math problem or assisting them with a research project. It is also likely that "fussing and fighting" is sometimes part of these interactions. My son, Ian, for example, is a good student, but we've still had our share of fights over homework. What I think was different for the parents I interviewed—parents whose children struggled with their schoolwork—was the frequency, intensity, and duration of these negative interactions. More to the point, taking on the role of their child's teacher was an important way that *school trouble* defined, at least partly, relationships between the parents and their children that were frustrating, tense, and denied parents and children opportunities to share more pleasurable activities together.

It might have been that some of these parents were frustrated because they lacked the skills to take on the role of their children's teachers. But even the parents I interviewed who were or had been classroom teachers—Tanya Wallace, Betty Springs, Edna Bunker, Elma Kinkead, Jamie Frick, David Thibault, Diane Riggs, and Maria Scott—reported similar frustrations and tensions when they tried to *help* their children with schoolwork. Maria Scott commented on how hard it was for her to teach school skills to her daughter.

> See I'm a day care teacher so I'm thinking to myself, she should be able to do this. I should have been able to teach her how to do this and how to do go about doing that. So I'm sitting there going to myself thinking: "What am I doing wrong? What can I do right?" I didn't know. It's a new thing for me.

So why was it so hard for the parents I interviewed to help their children with school work? Molly Reeves offered this analysis of the problem: "'Cause it's different if you're trying to teach your kid other than having someone else to teach him," she told me. "But, if you teach somebody else's kid, you know, you don't get aggravated." Even if parents know *how* to help their children with schoolwork, taking on the role of their child's teacher requires a redefinition of the parent-child relationship, at least for a time. Anyone who has ever tried to teach a family member to drive knows well the tensions that can emerge when family members attempt to step out of the parent-child or husband-wife role to the role of driving instructor. Taking on the roles of teacher and student involves family members in interactions, with particular kinds of expectations and behaviors, that often conflict with their roles and relationships within the family. If parents and/or children are unwilling to accept this shift in roles, even temporarily, tension and conflicts may result, as the above examples illustrate.

No wonder some parents tried explicitly to reject the role of being their child's teacher. Betty Springs, for example, recalled making a conscious decision to refuse the mother-as-teacher role with her son, Sam.

> I stopped being his teacher. I can't be his teacher. I have to be his mother. And I, what I did is, I backed off. I was on his case about his homework: "Have you got your homework done?" Remember you [referring to her husband] were at him because he was doing his homework in front of the TV? We were setting up all these rules for him and it didn't make it any better. All it did was cause friction in our family. It caused our family relationships to deteriorate. Finally I just thought, I'm not being your teacher any more. . . . I'll help him out if

he asks. But I'm not going to go and ride him about it. And I was rid-
ing him, you know. I was [also] trying to do all the things that I knew
his teachers weren't doing with him at school.

Betty Springs' assertion, "I can't be his teacher. I have to be his
mother" reinforces the sense that there is a natural tension when family members take on the role of teacher. But parents found that giv-
ing up the role of being their child's teacher was easier said than done
given the high stakes involved in schooling. Edna Bunker recalled once
telling her son, "The teachers are responsible for you. I'm not responsible for your education. You go and sit with the teacher until they help
you." "But it doesn't work," she told me. "The teachers don't have the
vested interest that I have. So it's not the same." It's not the same and
the stakes are too high for many parents to abandon responsibility for
their children's schoolwork. Elma Kinkead regretted all the arguments
she and her sixteen-year-old daughter, Andrea, had over grades, but
"academics present[ed] a long-term worry" to her that she couldn't ignore. So, like most of the parents I spoke to, Elma Kinkead resigned
herself to "fighting and fussing" with her daughter over schoolwork
even though she suspected it was damaging their relationship.

Time was also an issue in how school troubles defined parents' relationships with their children. The demands of homework, (sometimes
frequent) teacher conferences, phone calls from the school, driving
children to tutoring, and so on often left little time for parents and children to "have fun together," as Edna Bunker put it. Some parents,
however, did talk about how hard they worked to find spaces where
they could enjoy their children. Ralph Thorn had been actively involved in his children's Boy Scout troop when his sons were younger.
The Thibaults regularly took the whole family away for ski weekends
at their cottage. Before the Coopers removed their son, Peter, from
public school in favor of homeschooling, John Cooper sometimes took
Peter out of school so they could go fishing together. Other parents
were involved in their children's sports. Mr. McIsaac, for example, was
an assistant coach of his son's soccer team. But, based on the sample of
parents I interviewed, it was clearly difficult for these parents to find
the time to engage their children in pleasurable activities. This was especially true for single mothers who had to meet the demands of their
children's schooling and take care of domestic chores with little, if any,
help. Single moms were also denied the opportunity to find much relief from the emotionally charged interactions with their children
around schoolwork, as the following quote from single mother Betty
Blake illustrates.

I tend to yell a lot. I don't spank him, but I yell. I know that's not good
for him because I know that it is probably doing a lot of harm to his
self-esteem. I try not to yell, but I don't know what else to do because

it's not like I can say "Speak to your father." I have to try, I have to go
to work, do what is going on with work, and hear the school calling
me, then come home and try to talk to him and discipline him about
whatever it is that he's done that's wrong and it's overwhelming for
me. . . . I get so frustrated. I don't even know what to say any more.
Even tonight, doing that math. It just drives me crazy because I'll
spend half a day showing him how to do something and he'll know
how to do it as long as I'm sitting here. But if I move and say "do it on
your own," all of a sudden it's like "What?" He always wants me to be
there and I keep telling him that I'm not always going to be there. I'm
not in the class with you. You have to do it on your own. . . . He gets
very upset when I yell at him to the point where he cries. . . . I think
the fact that I get frustrated, it might have affected our relationship . . . [but] education is very important [so] I have yelled and
screamed until there was no tomorrow.

Jeb Moore talked about the difficulty of working with his son, Archie,
who "knows how to push my buttons" in much the same way that
Timmy Blake knew how to push his mother's "buttons"—another
problem for parents who take on the role of their children's teacher.
But in two-parent families there is at least the possibility of relief from
these situations.

Catherine Connor also spoke about her son's ability to engage her
in fights over his schoolwork, but, in her case, her stay-at-home husband assumed responsibility for their son's schoolwork. Amy Thibault
also acknowledged how difficult it was for her to work with her son
Steve, but her husband, David, assumed the primary responsibility for
Steve's schoolwork. Granted that many of the mothers in two-parent
households whom I talked to received no assistance from their husbands with their children's schoolwork, but there was at least the possibility for such support. Single mothers didn't even have the option of
telling their children to "speak to your father," as Betty Blake put it. I'll
have more to say about the burdens of school trouble on mothers in the
next chapter.

The tensions and frustrations over schoolwork also led some parents to (occasionally) resent their children for their part in their
struggles in school. Edna Bunker told me that she sometimes resented

all the time that [schoolwork] takes. I resent that I seem to have to
fight for him all the time. Going to teachers. [But] it's just what I have
to accept. I resent it, but that's the way it is. There is nothing I can do
about it so I just have to do it.

Sometimes parents directed these resentments toward their children. Celine Street, for example, talked about her response to teachers'
complaints about her son's behavior. "First of all, what goes through my
mind is: Why can't he just listen? Why can't he just sit down?" Carol
Dumay talked about her frustrations with her daughter's "attitude."

I have to find other avenues to get that pressure off of me. It does, it gets pretty bad sometimes when I see the attitude. 'Cause sometimes her attitude is like, "I don't care." That's what I think. But that may not be it. You know. It may not be . . . it's just that I feel that she don't care. She doesn't give it really that. . . . But I do some pushing. I have done a lot of pushing. I do have to push her a lot. But she has upset me a lot, where I felt I didn't like this child at all. Her attitude needs to be changed. . . . And I do have a feeling towards her like, maybe I shouldn't say I dislike her, but I just dislike her attitude. That's it, her attitude.

"Attitude" may have particularly been a problem for fathers. Joseph Riggs and James Wallace were among several fathers who, at one point or another, blamed their child's school troubles on "laziness." Andrea Kinkead did not live with her dad, yet, according to Mrs. Kinkead, his frequent complaints that Andrea's school troubles stemmed from her laziness eventually led Andrea to refuse to share anything about school with her father. Martin Springs had a more specific concern about his son's "attitude," in this case Sam's unwillingness to "play the game" of schooling. Sometimes he would think:

I don't need this hassle. I mean, I've got a job to do. I have things to do. Just play the game. Go to school. Get some good marks. Average marks, whatever. Don't get in trouble. You don't have to get into trouble. And let's go on. Hey, that's life too. It doesn't always work out that way.

Parents' involvement with their children's school troubles—through homework, surveilling grades and school assignments, contact with teachers, driving to tutoring, and so on—often created tense and frustrating relationships with their sons and daughters and, at the same time, made it difficult for them to find much time to engage their children in more pleasurable activities. In some cases, this led to resent their children, at least occasionally, for their role in school trouble.

For their part, children who struggled in school, in the minds of their parents at least, sometimes resented their parents' response to their school troubles, which they interpreted as rejection by their parents or, in the case of teenagers, as an unwelcome intrusion in their *private* lives.

"Momma, Do You Love Me?"

Elma Kinkead told me about the "colossal fights" she had with her sixteen-year-old daughter, Andrea, over report cards, report cards that "always included at least one A." Inevitably, according to Mrs. Kinkead, Andrea fought back by pointing out, "You never say anything about the A. You only talk about the other grades." Mrs. Kinkead felt that it was unnecessary to comment about the A on Andrea's report card because "that's what she's supposed to have." Perhaps, but many of the parents I interviewed acknowledged that their children resented the emphasis on what they didn't do well (i.e., poor grades). Mr. Moore, for example, talked about his son's anger over his parents' frequent corrections whenever he read to them. The Moores, like Ms. Kinkead, recognized the dangers of focusing on the *negative,* but their concerns over their children's academic futures made it difficult for them to do otherwise.

Some children also resented their parents' efforts to locate a cause for their difficulties in school, which suggested that there was something wrong with them. Edna Bunker, for example, actively explored the possibility that her son's troubles in school might be traceable to an attention deficit disorder (ADD) which could have, potentially, been treated with medication (Ritalin). Mrs. Bunker recalled watching a movie that focused on a family living with a child with an ADD. When she invited her son and husband to watch the movie with her, her son, Mike, "was defensive that I called him in, saying that you're always saying that there is something wrong with me." Mrs. Bunker continued, however, to collect information on ADD, first consulting her physician and then regularly attending group meetings for parents of children with ADD. She finally abandoned these efforts after an angry confrontation with her son. "I stopped going [to the ADD meetings] because Mike got so upset that I was 'labelling' him. I finally ripped up all the ADD information and told him, 'I'll never say you have ADD again.'"

My conversations suggested that diagnostic labels (e.g., learning disabled, ADD) were a comfort to many parents (I'll say more about this in Chapter 7). It may be, however, that other children felt as Mike did, that a label was emblematic of their parents' belief that there was something wrong with them.

Edna Bunker, like all the parents I met with, was ready and willing to do whatever was necessary to support her child's schooling, but, like other parents, her efforts weren't always welcomed. Teenagers, in particular, were especially likely to reject their parents' efforts to support their schooling. When Steve Thibault, for example, entered high school he would no longer accept his parents' help with school assignment and he began to respond angrily to their inquiries into his schoolwork. By eighth grade, Debbie Frick began to view her mother's involvement in her schooling—helping with homework, volunteering in Debbie's classroom, meeting with teachers and other school personnel to influence them to offer Debbie instructional opportunities best suited to her needs and (gifted) abilities, and so on—as unwelcome "interference." Here's how Jamie put it:

> By grade eight Mom was interfering. She didn't want me there . . . and she was becoming less open to telling me when things were going

wrong. Our dynamic was changing in grade eight. She didn't want Mom at school. . . . It was a fight. "You don't belong here." She had picked up on the culture that, by that time, it was clear enough that parents didn't participate in public school. . . . And she didn't want me to help her with her homework. She didn't want me to ask her questions at the end of the day. She wasn't offering information. It was sort of "Keep out of my life, Mom."

Debbie Frick's rejection of her mother's advocacy was a source of serious tension between them and hurt her mother deeply. Jamie is a single mother and Debbie is the focus of her life so she continued to talk to her daughter's teachers about methods and content that she believed failed to challenge her daughter sufficiently. Of course, this only exacerbated the tensions between them.

Children's rejection of their parents' involvement in their schooling was also hard on immigrant parents like Mrs. Ng, whose knowledge of North American schooling was limited. From Mrs. Ng's perspective, parent-teacher conferences were about the only way she had of making sense of her son's school experience. Yet, her thirteen-year-old son, Edward, got angry with her for going to these conferences which he claimed the parents of his friends did not attend.

There were exceptions to this pattern. Al and Ted Thorn—at least from their parents' perspective—welcomed their parents' advocacy in the face of unfair or disinterested teachers. Mr. Thorn believed that "our kids appreciate our involvement in their schooling and in the community [Boy Scouts, for example]. They are aware of the fights we have for them. . . ." Alice Mandel and Tanya Wallace also indicated that their daughters accepted their support willingly. But these parents still reported significant tensions over homework with their daughters and sons.

The resentment and anger that emerged from parents' and children's interactions around schooling led some children to question their parents' love and affection. Betty Blake often worried, she said, that the anger she sometimes expressed over frustrating homework sessions with her son "might have affected [their] relationship." Carol Dumay was stung when her daughter questioned her love.

> She'd say, "Do you love me?" I'd say, "We love you no matter what. . . . We try to help you to do better so you could go on a lead a more productive life. She doesn't quite understand that at ten [years old]. Anyway she feels, I think, that sometimes that we don't care about her. [Talking about her brothers and sisters] "You like them, you don't like me. Because they do better in this, they do better in that." I don't want her to feel like that. I keep thinking that maybe I don't . . . no matter what now, I have to find out something like this so I want to know the right things to say to her so that she won't feel like that. I don't know

how she feels sometimes. I talk to her, but I'm not quite sure she understands, because of that loving part [when] she says, "Do you love me?" I worry about her a lot. I worry about her a lot.

My daughter, Anne, bristled with anger when she recalled the use of "homework books" when she was in elementary school (see Chapter 1). "Only the stupid kids had homework books so, if I had a homework book, I must be stupid. . . . *The homework books made me feel that even my parents thought I was stupid.*" As we found with homework books, parents' interventions in support of their children's schooling can be a two-edged sword. Helping children with their homework, intervening with teachers, and so on provide children who struggle in school with needed support. At the same time, however, this *help* can engage parents and children in negative interactions that undermine parent-child relationships and may lead (some) children to question how much their parents care about them. Few, if any, of the parents I interviewed would be willing to withdraw their support for their children's schooling even if some, like David Thibault and Betty Springs, contemplated this possibility. But I'm sure most of the parents shared the concern expressed by Betty Blake about the effect of school trouble on her long-term relationship with her son. Their interactions over homework were, she feared, damaging their relationship, but the stakes were too high for her to ignore her son's schoolwork.

Given the complex interdependence of relationships within families, it seems likely that the frustrations and tensions over school trouble would spill over into other family relationships and not just the interactions between parents and children who struggled in school. This was certainly the case among the parents I interviewed as I document in the next section.

"The Only Thing We Fight About Are Those Kids."

One of the most stressful aspects of my daughter, Anne's, struggles in school was its effect on my relationship with my wife (see Chapter 1). Anger and frustration over Anne's schooling often spilled over into our relationship and there were bitter arguments over how best to respond to Anne's problems at school. Although we learned to manage our anger and disagreements, we never found complete relief from the stress of school troubles on our marriage until Anne started doing (relatively) well in school. So I was particularly interested in the effect of school trouble on the marriages of the parents I interviewed and I usually asked parents explicitly about the impact of school trouble on their relationships with their spouses. Not surprisingly, many parents were not particularly forthcoming about stories of marital strife with a stranger, even if these conflicts were in the past. Some of the parents I interviewed did, however, at least acknowledge occasional tensions related to school trouble. Mr. Cooper recalled how his wife sometimes got angry with him for being insensitive about the way he talked to their son "who already felt bad that he didn't read as fast as I wanted him to read." Mr. McIsaac, although dismissing any suggestions of marital stress over their son's problems, conceded that there were occasional tensions in their house over the fact that he didn't always acknowledge the fact that his wife bore most of the burdens of homeschooling (their response to school trouble). The "sharing" of responsibility for the additional demands imposed by their son, Mike's, struggles in school was also a source of conflict between Edna Bunker and her husband, Sheldon.

> When you've got somebody to worry about, if everything's going great with the rest of your life, it's not so much strain. But I was doing a lot of blaming last year because Sheldon was supposed to be coming home at 3:30 and monitoring Mike's [schoolwork] and I felt like he wasn't doing it. I felt like I had to be home and that's why I feel like I have to be home this year [instead of getting a job]. I feel like we're not in this equally. Our concerns are not equal. But Sheldon wouldn't say that. He would say, he's just as concerned as I am. To me, he doesn't show it. I have resentment towards him because of that. . . . We just fought a lot. We had lots of fights. And that's when we went to family counseling, because we had all these fights. [Last year] was not a happy year, I don't think, for anybody.

Betty and Martin Springs also talked specifically about the effect of school trouble on their relationship. Mrs. Springs told me: "We don't fight. The only thing we fight about are these kids." One of the things they fought about, for example, was how to present themselves in meetings with Sam's teachers.

> A specific example [of conflict] would be preparation for going into a meeting with Sam's teachers. We'd talk about the kinds of things we could say that wouldn't get the teachers' backs up, but still support Sam. Martin would say, "I'm just saying this, this, this" and I would say, "You can't say that!" Because then the teachers are going to dump all over Sam afterwards. And we would go in to the meeting and Martin would get really frustrated and he would just say this, this, and this. Then I would be upset with him afterwards: "You shouldn't have said this. You shouldn't have said that." And we were coming home from these meetings and we were going at each other about, "Well I had to say this." "You shouldn't have said that." Then we would be tense about it.

Still, Mrs. Springs tried to minimize the tension they experienced over Sam's struggles at school. When I asked her if "the tensions were that serious," she indicated, "No, not between Martin and I." Yet, this apparently wasn't how their son saw it. From Sam's perspective these episodes seemed much more serious. Sam told his father, "I hate it when you guys fight. I hate it!" His level of concern was evident in the question he asked his mother: "Are you guys going to get a divorce over this?"

For the Springs, school trouble meant conflict over Martin Springs' deportment at conferences with Sam's teachers. For Cybil and Ralph Thorn, the issue of labeling was the source of tension. Mr. Thorn had this to say about arguments he and his wife had over the meaning of labels.

> So every label she was picking up, she was automatically slapping the worst connotation on to it. "Oh they are going to go through this; they're not going to be able to make a living; they're not going to be able to get a degree; they're not going to be able to get by in school; they're going to have trouble; they're not going to be able to function in society." The worst case scenario. . . . I rebelled against this and we had some violent arguments because I said, "Just because the kids have difficulty in learning and learned it a different way, doesn't make them any worse."

The amount of time that mothers spent helping struggling children could also a source of friction for some couples. Carol Dumay, for example, felt that her husband resented all the time she spent doing schoolwork with their daughter, denying him of time he wanted to spend with his wife.

> My husband blamed me, "You shouldn't sit there so much. Let her alone, on her own." "Why do you sit there with her night after night and go through that?" And I thought that I had to. But he didn't think that I should. So that was a lot of tension between us two.

When I asked Mrs. Dumay why it bothered her husband when she worked with her daughter, she speculated, "Maybe it was taking a tantrum, I believe. I do believe that. But I told him, 'She needs help.'"

The financial demands of school trouble were also contentious for Mrs. Dumay and her husband. Mrs. Dumay talked, for example, about her husband's resistance to taking their daughter, Georgina, to the Sylvan Learning Center for testing and tutoring.

> The Sylvan Learning Center goes back to when the problem starts, where they think it does, and they work from there. But that costs like $100 just to have her tested. . . . That's not too bad. I would have spent that, but my husband said, "No." He didn't think that she needed that

type of thing. So I said, "Okay." But sometimes there is a little conflict between me and him about what she needs. I'm willing to take the money. But he's like, "Hold up. Hold up. Is that necessary? You think she needs that? I don't know about that." So we have a little [tiff] and it ends up that we don't do it.

Interestingly, Molly Reeves, one of the single mothers I talked to, suggested that it was an advantage not having to negotiate decisions over her son's schooling with his father. However, Ms. Reeves made it clear that divorce didn't necessarily end conflicts over child rearing. She had this to say about the burdens of being a single mother:

> Oh, it's rough. It's real rough. Because it's like I'm the bad guy. [My kids say] "You make me do homework. You make me go to school. You make me clean my room. I gotta wash my hands. I gotta brush my teeth. I gotta take a shower." Last summer I let their dad keep them for about two months. And he didn't help them [with their reading]. I told him, make sure they read, 'cause I got all kinds of books. And the kids, I said, get them books out and read them through the summer. They swore they would. But their dad didn't even get the books out. He did nothing. They just rode jeeps, went fishing and camping and things like that. They didn't even try to do any reading through the whole summer. So this summer, he isn't getting them. When they're with him they have all kinds of fun. They have fun fishing and stuff like that. And it makes me feel that they think I'm the bad guy and he's the hero.

On the face of it, there is nothing particularly out of the ordinary about the kind of marital tensions these parents described. All couples fight, at least occasionally, and disputes over money, the sharing of domestic responsibilities, and issues of child rearing are fairly routine in many households. I also suspect that it is not unusual for husbands to sometimes resent competing with their children for their wives' attention. But the stakes over schooling are high as most parents link success in school with their children's life chances (e.g., good schools, good jobs, and so on). It is my impression—based on these interviews and my own experience—that this contributes to a frequency and intensity of friction between spouses that may be out of the ordinary. For many of students who struggle in school, it appears that marital tension is just one more burden. Still, Mr. and Mrs. Thorn, while recalling "violent arguments" over their son's troubles in school, also believed that fighting for their children's interests strengthened the bond between them. The McIsaacs shared this point of view. Perhaps external pressures can sometimes bring couples closer together, but the stresses of school trouble—fear for children's future, demands on scarce time and financial resources, the thwarting of expectations, and so on—will almost certainly make it more difficult for couples to maintain warm, loving, and supportive relationships, something that isn't always easy under the best of circumstances. Although they were reluctant to say so, I'm certain many of the parents I interviewed would agree with Carol Dumay, who said her daughter's struggles in school routinely created a "lot of tensions" between her and her husband.

The *Other* Child

Parents also talked to me about the impact of school trouble on their relationships with their *other* children, sons and daughters who did not struggle in school. Betty Springs, for example, admitted that, like any parent, she sometimes took out frustrations she experienced over one child—in this case, her son—on her daughter, which her daughter resented. "One time I asked my daughter to do something and I was really sharp with her and she shot back, 'Don't dump all over me because Sam's having trouble at school. It's not my fault.'"

More often school trouble meant less time for spending with *other* children or minimizing their accomplishments. Diane Chu explained that her younger daughter was often jealous of all the time she spent with her older daughter, the one diagnosed with "language disabilities," on homework. Similarly, Diane Riggs talked about the challenge of supporting her son who struggled in school and still having enough time to help her other children with their homework.

> What happens is [my younger son] Ben needs my help as well and [my older daughter] Esther needs my help as well. My husband is at work for long hours so I'm really by myself at night with them doing their homework. I don't give equal time to my children and it's Ben who is suffering because he seems to be able to pick it up very quickly, But I'm looking over what he is doing and helping him as much as I should. And Esther needs a lot more help in mathematics and I've let that slide.

Mrs. Riggs added, "It's always a juggle no matter what, you know, [even] if you have three perfect children, you'd still be doing that." "Juggling" the needs of children is much more difficult, however, when one of those children requires significant amounts of parents' time to get along in school.

Single mother Celine Street paid a particularly high price for her inability to juggle the needs of her children to her older son's satisfaction. "Like it wasn't just with Dennis. . . . I still had my older son Russell. . . . He resented me because I was focusing so much on Dennis, you know, trying to teach him." The impossibility of meeting Dennis's *and* Russell's needs eventually led Russell to move in with his father.

Several parents also talked to me about the "need" to minimize the accomplishments of children who did well in school out of consideration for the feelings of children for whom school was a struggle. This often led to resentment toward the sibling who struggled academically. Betty Springs talked about the complications of recognizing her daughter's superior achievements without hurting the feelings of her son, Sam.

> It caused problems for Cindy because what was happening is, she does so well in school and she was coming home on the honor role and we're going, "Shhh! We'll talk about it later." She's really good and she understands what Sam is going through and she appreciates our position. But she said to me one time, "It's really frustrating for me, Mom. I'm doing really well and we have to pretend that's not happening." And she was right. She was absolutely right . . . and it's caused a fair bit of tension.

David Thibault joked about feeling constrained in his and his wife's ability to acknowledge their younger son's school achievements.

> You wonder about whether or not, how much of a deal do you make, when Mark comes home and his report card is good. How much do you say, "This is the best report card we've ever seen. Finally, we've got a kid who knows how to read! Everybody, look here! Read to us, Mark!" I mean, you can't make so much out of Mark's good performance because [of Steve's struggles].

Based on my conversations with parents, it seems that the presence of a brother or sister who struggles in school affects both the quality and quantity of attention other siblings receive from their parents. For their part, struggling students often had to cope with the reality of siblings whose excellent school achievement only heightened their own sense of failure. For these reasons alone, I wouldn't have been surprised to have heard lots of stories of resentment and conflict among siblings, but this was not how their parents saw it. The experiences of the parents I interviewed were similar, I think, to Tanya Wallace's perceptions of her children's relationship. At time of our interview, Mrs. Wallace's two children, Catherine and Brian, were fourteen and seventeen. Brian excelled in school, while Catherine struggled. Still, Mrs. Wallace had this to say about their relationship.

> People talk about having two teenagers, the fact that they fight a lot. These two argue sometimes, but really they are very supportive of each other. They're very good with each other. They nag at each other, but when it comes right down to it, when the chips are down for one, the other one is right there. . . . [When Catherine was depressed about school] Brian would ask, "How is Catherine doing? Is she feeling bet-

ter, do you think?" They kind of watch out for each other. He, I think, he's empathetic.

Mrs. Wallace also believed that Brian's experience with his sister's struggles in school helped him develop more empathy toward children who did poorly with academic work in his own class.

I was also interested in the possible effects of school troubles on extended family relationships. It's not hard to imagine, for example, tension between parents and grandparents over child rearing decisions, especially in the case of "problems," like school failure. However, single mother Celine Street was the only parent I interviewed who had much to say about this. Celine's relationships with her family were strained because of her siblings' unwillingness to help her cope with raising a son with attention deficit disorder (ADD)[1] by herself. Basically, she felt she had to deal with Dennis alone, even though she had extended family in the area.

> I have absolutely no support with him. Since Dennis was a year and a half, I've never had any time away from him. Never. I've never had any one of them [her brother or two sisters] take him for a weekend to give me a break or baby-sit him for any length of time. My sister basically refuses to take him overnight because, when he was about five . . . she watched him on a Saturday afternoon and he stayed overnight because I had to leave for work very early [Sunday morning]. . . . Before my sister woke up, Dennis got up, got dressed, went out of the apartment and started walking home . . . and he tried to cross a very busy intersection. . . . At that point she said, "Don't ever ask me to watch him overnight again." Anytime I ask them to baby-sit him for a few hours at a time so I could go away, maybe do something a few hours every week or something, they refuse. They say, "No, we are not going to watch him. Absolutely not."

Celine's brother and two sisters refused to even offer her sympathy for her situation. Her mother was more sympathetic but, because she lived more than one thousand miles away, she was unable to provide Celine with anything beyond moral support.

Among the families I interviewed, each and every family member—mothers, fathers, brothers, and sisters—seem to have been affected by school trouble as were relationships among family members. The evidence suggests, however, that the burden of having a child who struggled in school fell most heavily upon mothers. This is the subject of the next chapter.

---

[1] Attention deficit disorder is often overdiagnosed, but even the most casual observer would have agreed that her Celine's son Dennis was an extremely active, distractible, and demanding child.

Chapter Six

School Troubles
A Mother's Burden

*When you have a child who has problems with reading, you have
something that's hurt, torn out.*
                    —Interview with Carol Dumay

One of the mothers I interviewed observed that her parents didn't offer
much support for her schooling when she as a child. "It didn't seem that
parents did it in those days," she told me. But things were different
now, she believed.

> In the 1990s, it seems that parents are more involved with what their
> kids are doing. Like my parents couldn't have cared less . . . like every-
> thing was left up to the school. But it's different now, it seems.

Indeed, things may be different now. Prior to the 1960s, there were few
indications that teachers expected (or even wanted) parents to take an
active role in their children's schooling. Although I do not think that
parents care any more about their children or their children's schooling than they used to, there is evidence that, over the last thirty years
or so, parents are more involved in their children's lives at school. At
the end of the twentieth century, mothers—and, to a lesser degree,
fathers—are much more likely, and expected, to be actively involved in
their children's school careers (Lareau 1989). However, *parent involvement* more often refers to the work of women in support of their chil-

dren's schooling (Griffith 1996) as the domestic role of mothers has expanded to include responsibility for their children's cognitive development and schooling (Baker and Stevenson 1986). According to educational researcher Annette Lareau (1989), the coordination and supervision of children's educational activities often demands a significant portion of mothers' waking hours, particularly in the case of mothers whose children are doing poorly in school. This work typically includes: monitoring children's school standing; communicating with teachers; helping children organize their time to do homework; helping them with homework itself; and, in the case of children who have difficulty in school, taking some action to remedy the problem (Griffith and Smith, 1990).

Among the parents I interviewed, school troubles had a significant impact on the lives of both mothers and fathers. Mothers *and* fathers felt the pain of children who suffered through failure at school. Mothers *and* fathers both felt the pinch of financial sacrifices that often resulted from the cost of academic testing, tutoring, and private schools. Mothers *and* fathers were affected by the loss of income when mothers left the workplace to homeschool their children or, in the case of Edna Bunker, postponed working outside the home so that she could devote all of her time to supporting her son's schooling. Nor could any parent escape the family tensions that always surround school trouble. Sometimes mothers and fathers shared the material burdens of school trouble—that is, helping children with their homework, talking with teachers, driving children to tutoring, and so on—and, as I discussed in the last chapter, at least two of the fathers assumed the primary responsibility for schoolwork. But, among the parents I interviewed, mothers carried a disproportionate share of the *emotional* and *material* burdens of having a child who struggled in school. Overwhelmingly, school trouble was a mother's burden and, in this chapter, I focus on the physical and psychological work performed by mothers to cope with having children for whom school was a struggle.

"The Teachers Can't Do Enough."

Edna Bunker explained her extraordinary efforts in support of her son's schooling with this simple observation: "The teachers can't do enough." So, like the other mothers I interviewed, Mrs. Bunker tried to do what she believed her son's teachers were not able to do: provide intensive, frequent individualized support for her son's schooling. None of the mothers was as overburdened by the demands of school trouble, however, as single mother Celine Street, whose son Dennis had been diagnosed as ADD. Providing for Dennis's needs placed nearly overwhelming demands on Celine's time. Here is what Celine had to say when I asked her if she was able to find any time for her needs.

> None. No, I don't have time. My whole life is focused on Dennis. I have no other life. Absolutely none. If I do go somewhere, I have to think of something to do with Dennis. I have to think about where I am going because I am taking Dennis with me and the whole time that I am there, if it is with my family [for example], it's very tension filled. Because he doesn't listen, because he is running around. And they get upset at him, because he is not listening. And I get upset. . . .

Celine's description of her daily domestic routine provides ample evidence to support her claim that she has almost "no life" beyond Dennis.

> We're up at 5:30 in the morning. We're out of here by a quarter to seven. . . . It's come down to a routine. We get up at a certain hour and I say this and there's no fooling around with Dennis 'cause he'd do absolutely nothing. . . . [But] it's still an argument to this day. . . . [Then] I take him to a sitter. The sitter is across from the school. At 8:30 he leaves and goes to school [and] I'm already at work. . . . I'm at work by 8:00. . . . I get home from the [commuter] train and I pick him up and I come home. So there's never any interim time there, when I'm without him. The only time I get a break is when I am at work and on the train, which is when I do my reading, because it's a half hour there and a half hour back. So that's my time. That's the only time I get to myself.

Dennis dominated her time, but Celine still felt that her domestic responsibilities prevented her from spending a sufficient amount of time with her son. She worried, for example, that she didn't spend enough time helping Dennis with his schoolwork.

> I know if I spend time with Dennis to do anything, he would do it very well. Unfortunately, this is, you know, a problem a lot of the time. It is about 6:00 . . . by the time I pick him up at the sitter and come home. And then I'm stuck with this. I have my routine to do. I have to come home and feed him. I've got to clean up. I have other things. I have to go shopping to buy some things during the week or I have to do my laundry. By the time we hit 8:00, it's too late. He's too tired. He goes to bed at 8:30. If Dennis doesn't get enough sleep he's very, very cranky. . . . I know that I need to spend time with him and I do, but during the week he knows that I can't do these kind of things. You come home, you cook, you clean, you do all these other things. We can sit and watch TV for about half an hour. This is our time together.

On top of the routine demands, Celine also dealt with phone calls from Dennis' teachers and it seemed that there had been lots of phone calls from Dennis' teachers, even calling Celine at work, to complain about his behavior. Then there were conferences with teachers at Dennis' school, visits to the doctor's office, monitoring Dennis' medication, and on and on. At the time I interviewed Celine Street, Dennis was only in third grade so he still didn't have much homework. Based on the experience of the other parents I talked to (see Chapter 4), it's likely that the demands of homework were going to make Celine's stressful life even more stressful.

Although Dennis consumed most of her time Celine did find a little time for herself after Dennis went to bed even if she sometimes felt guilty for "stealing" this time from Dennis.

> This is my time. I need an hour to myself, to calm down, to go to sleep myself. This is how I have managed the time so I don't affect Dennis although he makes me feel guilty quite a bit of the time for doing this. I tell myself, no, I can't let him do this to me because this is the only time I have. . . . You were asking how does his school affect how I am at home. The only way I can deal with it is by doing this specifically, by having my time on the [commuter] train to myself and then I have my time when he goes to bed. That's for me to do with my time. And that's what I look forward to really.

Celine also found a little time to herself by "pretending to sleep in until 11:00 on Saturday mornings" while Dennis watched television. But time out of the house, beyond traveling to and from her job on a commuter train, was nearly impossible for her to arrange for financial reasons (recall from the previous chapter the unwillingness of Celine's family to offer her any relief from Dennis). This is what she had to say when I asked her if she "ever used baby-sitters to get yourself some relief."

> I can't afford it . . . I don't have the money to spare on that. A lot of people say, well it's for your sanity, [but] I really can't. I tried it a few times and I can't. I like doing things like darts and bowling and all that kind of stuff. And, for a while, I tried getting out every Tuesday night. My sitter would cost me almost $10 because I'd be gone from about 7:00 to 9:30 at three dollars an hour . . . so it cost me an average of $10 a week plus what I spent when I was out. So we are talking between $50 and $60 per month. To a lot of people that's not very much. To a person who has to live on a budget, $20 a month makes a big difference, maybe the difference between paying the phone bill or not. . . . I pay for the sitter [in the morning]. I work downtown. It costs me a fortune to take the train. [Celine lives far from her job because of the high cost of housing in Megacity.] I'm surprised I'm not on social assistance. I count myself one of the lucky ones to have enough money to do this. But just barely. And in-between that I am fighting with my ex-husband to make sure that he gives me my money every month.

Celine Street was a good and caring mother who would never have characterized her son or his "problems" as a burden. Certainly, she would have liked some relief from the relentless demands of being a single mother with a son who required nearly constant vigilance and a firm hand. As she herself put it, "Dennis wears people down," and I suspect that included his mother.

Still, the only thing unique about Celine Street's experience among the mothers I interviewed was its intensity. All of the single moms I talked to described domestic routines nearly as demanding as Celine's. Betty Blake, for example, responded to my comment that "being a single mother doesn't leave you a lot of time," by observing:

> Oh, no it doesn't. Oh, we're on a strict routine. We walk through that door at 6:00. He goes into the shower. While he's in the shower I'm getting dinner ready. When he comes out of the shower, he lotions his skin, puts on his pajamas and, if the table's not set, he sets the table. Or he starts his homework if he has homework and the dinner's not ready. Like, we're on a strict routine. That's right. So that eating and homework are finished by 8:30. The latest.

Betty Blake, like most of the parents I interviewed, believed that it was important that her son have a life beyond school so she enrolled him in karate on Mondays, a Heritage Language Program on Saturdays, and church on Sunday—all of which made additional demands on her time.

Single mother Molly Reeves also described a family life that left her little time for herself.

> I make them go to bed at nine. But when they go to bed, I got to get up and get all my cleaning and stuff done. Pick up this. Pick up that. And I go to bed. I can't watch news, you know. I can't sit up late. I get up at 5:00 and I can't, the latest I've sat up in I don't know how long, is about 10:30.

When I interviewed Molly, she was attending school to work toward her GED as a state-imposed requirement for receiving public assistance, but found that the demands of organizing the household and supporting her sons' schoolwork left her little time for her own homework as illustrated by the following exchange.

CDM: I get the impression that when the kids are home from school, you spend a good chunk of your time on their homework.

Molly: On homework and helping them read the little books [assigned by the university reading clinic].

CDM: That doesn't give you much time to relax, even to do your work.

Molly: No, because I supposed to do my homework, but yet I can't do it because I run out of time by helping my son. And then by the time I get my share of stuff taken care of, 'cause I get up at 5:00 like I said, then I'm ready to go to bed. I'm foolin' with that. I'll do [my homework] at school.

CDM: So you don't get your homework done.

Molly: No. Mostly, no.

School trouble created other demands for parents, which single mothers had to shoulder themselves[1]. When Maria Scott's daughter, Tiffany, began to struggle in school Maria sought out alternatives, once spending the night waiting in line to get her daughter a spot in one of the school district's magnet schools. When Tiffany's poor school performance continued in the magnet school, Maria struggled to find the time between her job in a day care center and taking classes at the university, where she was working on a bachelor's degree, to visit schools that might be suitable for her daughter. Nor did Maria Scott have anyone with whom to share the responsibility of taking her daughter to her weekly tutoring at the university reading clinic or to karate or other after school activities. When I suggested that it must be very hard to meet these demands, she agreed and explained, "because I'm by myself . . . doing everything by myself."

Still, single mothers were not the only moms who seemed to cope with the demands of coping with school trouble by "doing everything" themselves.

"I Feel That I Do More of It Than Him."

In two-parent families, there is at least the potential for mothers to get some relief from domestic chores—including supporting children's schoolwork. And, among the families I interviewed, there were several fathers who took on at least some of the responsibility for supporting children's schoolwork. Martin Springs, John Mandel, and Ralph Thorn, for example, were among the fathers who routinely attended teacher conferences with their wives. John Cooper and Jeb Moore were only two of the fathers who said they "did their best" to help their children with homework even if it frequently taxed their patience. And, of course, two of the fathers—David Thibault and Catherine Connor's husband, George—assumed almost total responsibility for their children's schooling. Still, with these notable exceptions, the mothers in my sample did not get much help from their husbands supporting their children's schoolwork. Rosa Jones, for example, got no help from her

---

[1] I don't doubt that single fathers shoulder the same burdens as single mothers. My sample did not, however, include any single fathers.

husband with their children's schoolwork. "He ain't interested," she told me. Rosa went on:

> With homework and when it comes to the children, I feel single because my husband works a lot of hours. Sometimes he goes in at 6:00 in the morning and doesn't get off until 9:00 at night and sometimes he works his regular shift and he has to get up at 2:00 in the morning, go in, and break down the car wash and put new parts in and stuff like that. And then get through and work his regular shift.

Although I cannot speak for Rosa Jones's husband, I believe that it is a rare father who isn't interested in the education of their children. It's just that in mainstream North American culture domestic chores—and in our culture supporting children's schooling counts as a domestic chore—are primarily the responsibility of mothers. Janet Moore, for example, takes her son to tutoring, works with him on his homework, and is generally responsible for her children's schoolwork "If you want testing or anything done, I'm the one who takes him" [and if the teachers call] "I'm the one who ends up talking to them for an hour or two." This was all said without any apparent resentment in the presence of her husband, who did not disagree. Similarly, it was Edna Bunker, not her husband, Sheldon, who monitored their son's homework, met with teachers, and gathered materials for his assignments. "I guess we share," she told me, "but I feel I do more of it than him." And this was generally the pattern among the mothers I interviewed who did "more of it" than their husbands.

Arguably, Janet Moore and Edna Bunker were stay-at-home moms who might be expected to assume most of their family's domestic responsibilities. But the pattern of domestic responsibilities did not seem much different in families where mothers worked outside of the home. Alice Mandel held a demanding job as the director of a social service agency, but, because she has a background in education, her husband assumed that she would take charge of their daughter's homework, meet with teachers, and so on. "My husband says," she told me, "it's your field. You know what to do."

But the expectation that schoolwork is mothers' work did not change in homes where mothers were not as expert about education as Alice Mandel. Michelle Phills had a full-time job and no background in education, but she spent enormous amounts of her time searching for appropriate services for her daughter, Joy, and doing whatever she could to persuade school personnel to provide an education that met Joy's needs. Diane Riggs worked part-time in her husband's business, but still found the time to volunteer regularly in their children's school, manage their children's homework, and organize tutoring for their son and daughter. Her comment, "It is very difficult to get out in the evening to do something for myself," recalled what I heard from single mothers. Cybil Thorn characterized the work she did meeting with her sons' teachers, consultants, and the principal and as an active member of the school council and the district association for students with learning disabilities as a "second full-time job." Perhaps the most extraordinary example of mothers balancing their domestic responsibilities with work outside the home was Marilyn Cooper. At the time I interviewed Mrs. Cooper she was homeschooling two of her children and working outside the home (she left for work as soon as her husband returned home around 4:00). Arguably, Marilyn Cooper managed three full-time jobs: teacher, homemaker, and nurse.

As hard as these mothers worked to maintain their households and support their children's schooling, few of them felt that their efforts were sufficient. "You feel that you're not doing enough for your child," is how Rosa Jones put it. And it was this emotional burden—the subject of the next section—that really set the mothers I interviewed apart from fathers.

"I've Cried a Thousand Times."

Among the mothers I interviewed, the emotional costs of school troubles were high. This is what Betty Springs, for example, had to say about the psychological effects of her teenage son's struggles in school.

> I wasn't sleeping. It consumes you when you are afraid, when you are so afraid for your kid. It consumes you and you feel so useless and there's not anything you can do. Like we tried to do everything we could do. . . . I was angry. I was scared. I was terrified. I thought, "What's going to happen?" And it was frustrating for us both because we thought, "This is a really great kid. And [his teachers aren't] seeing this. They saw him as a glass half empty, not as a glass half full. . . . I remember waking up one night, it was about 3:00 in the morning. I'd been reading something in [an educational journal] about minority students and what's ahead for a lot of those kids. I remember thinking I knew that intellectually, but I [suddenly] knew how those moms felt, that when their kids are going into school, maybe before they even get there, there's a really good chance that they're not going to succeed. And I thought, God, that's how those women feel. That's how I was feeling about Sam. It didn't matter what I did, it wasn't going to make any difference for him. Like [his teachers] have made up their minds about him. In the high school they have decided where he fits on the bell curve, and that's where he's going to be.

When I asked Betty about the degree to which these feelings dominated her life, she made it clear that there was no time during the day when she was able to escape completely feelings of sadness, anger, frustration, and anxiety.

> I couldn't focus. I was trying to write a paper [for a graduate course]. I couldn't focus on it. I couldn't maintain my attention. I know for a fact that the students I was working with this year didn't get all of me that I gave them two years before. It just didn't seem quite as important to me after that. I wasn't sleeping. I wasn't eating. I was worrying constantly.

To illustrate the physical effect worrying over school trouble was having, she added that one of the secretaries at her school had commented on her weight loss (from not eating).

When I was a student at the University of Cincinnati, we studied the emotional impact of being a parent of children with moderate to severe learning problems and learned that having a child with serious physical and/or cognitive handicaps can be emotionally devastating. What parents like Betty Springs demonstrate is that, in a culture that places a premium on school achievement, even relatively mild problems at school—and Sam wasn't actually failing any of his school subjects—is incredibly stressful for parents, especially mothers. Nor was Betty Springs alone in her feelings of distress. The following excerpt from my interview with Maria Scott echoes many of the themes raised by Betty Springs.

CDM: Did your worries affect your school work? [Maria was taking night courses at the local university.]

Maria: It made it very hard. I didn't have time to study because I was thinking about her troubles in school. She's my first priority.

CDM: Did it affect your work as well?

Maria: In some ways, yeah. Because sometimes I didn't want to get up and go in to work if I was worrying. I wasn't getting so much sleep. So it's like I didn't want to be here.

CDM: So you lost sleep?

Maria: Yeah, yeah thinking about that. Like I said, this is my only child so it's like you want to mold your child a certain way . . . and when something goes wrong it hits you. It hits you hard.

CDM: How often were you losing sleep?

Maria: Mostly every night. Especially when they told me she might have an attention deficit disorder and she couldn't read. I thought, my child? It was hard . . . I'd wake up maybe about three o'clock in the morning, wake up and stay up until around four and then I had to be at work at six o'clock. It was hard for me just thinking how's the day going to go. Am I going to get a call from the teacher? Is her report card going to be this way or that way? I would just worry about it. Like I said you want your best for your kid, you want your child to do best, do good. And when they are not doing good, it's hard.

Maria Scott, like Betty Springs, found that her worries intruded on her work and, among the mothers who worked outside the home, this was a common reaction to school trouble. At one point Betty Blake's work-day was dominated by her fear that the school was going to call her at work—again.

> I lived in fear at work. I lived in fear and prayed when I got to work that I would not get a call from the school. That's how bad it was. I prayed every day for the school not to call. Every time I saw my lights flashing on my phone, I was afraid it was the school.

Mothers were particularly concerned for their children's future. Edna Bunker, for example, worried about how her son would fare in high school.

> I'm scared for high school. I'm just scared that he won't get the indi-vidual attention that he really needs. And I'm scared because I don't know anyone over there. I know everyone over at the elementary school. It scares me. . . . I'm thinking that he won't do great in ninth grade. It's like I'm gearing myself up already. I'm gearing myself up for ninth grade to sort of lower my expectations. It's a change of school and he doesn't do well with changes, so if he can just get through the year, and I'm thinking that should be enough. It's more like I'm just gearing myself up.

"Gearing up" for the future made for a very stressful present for many of the mothers I interviewed. But it was life in the present that was most troubling for mothers, particularly the effects school trouble was having on their children. Struggling in school made their children unhappy and no parent wants to see their child suffer. Sheila McIsaac echoed a theme I heard frequently from mothers.

> I'm just trying to look back. . . . Oh, it was terrible. It was a nightmare. It was a nightmare to see a little kid, to see . . . there were days that were good and there were days that were bad. But it was very sad. It's sad to see your child going [through that]. You love this kid and you try to do everything you can for them and you see them off to school and they go off in the morning and you know that they're gone all day, and you see them go off and they're so miserable like a puppy with its tail between its legs. They just looked so forlorn and lost. And you think they are going to spend the whole day there like that. I know there's periods of the day where they are probably quite happy and they're having good fun with their friends, and it's not as bad as you think, but it just seemed like an awful waste of time to see them go off so unhappy. It was terrible. It was a nightmare to see them go off and know they weren't achieving anything, they weren't getting anything positive out of the day. All those hours in that day. That was disturbing.

I began this chapter by citing cultural expectations that, since the second world war, the domestic work of mothers had expanded to include schoolwork. Given the expectation that schoolwork *equals* women's work, many readers may not find it surprising that mothers often felt responsible when their children struggled at school. But it was guilt over their children's troubles at school that clearly set mothers apart from fathers in my interviews. Mothers may have been more likely to take responsibility for helping their children with homework or meeting with teachers, but some fathers also helped with homework and met with teachers. Mothers may also have been more likely to worry or lose sleep over their children's struggles in school, but fathers also expressed worry and I, for one, have lost more than a little sleep worrying over my daughter's school troubles. Mothers appeared to be alone, however, in their willingness to blame themselves for their children's struggles at school. There may be fathers for whom school trouble leads to feelings of guilt, but none of the fathers I spoke to blamed themselves for their children's problems in school. Several fathers did, according to the mothers I interviewed, blame their wives, however.

"I Do Feel Like It Was My Fault. . . ."

It made me feel that I wasn't raising my child properly. It was *my* fault. It was something I did.

—Interview with Celine Street

Perhaps because I am a man, there was nothing about my interviews that surprised me more than the willingness of literally every mother I interviewed to accept the blame for their children's problems in school. Elma Kinkead, for example, was quick to take her daughter's school troubles as evidence of her poor parenting skills. "There's an element of guilt," she told me,

> I wonder if [my daughter's] poor performance is a reflection of my poor performance as a mother because I'm not taking time to do certain things because I am busy doing whatever it is that I have been doing. . . . I think that in between the yelling and screaming [other mothers] say wonderful things about their children to their friends but I don't say anything wonderful about my child. . . . I don't think I'm a good mother. I either should have had more than one [child] or none.

Carol Dumay also attributed her daughter's struggles in school to her own *failure* in "bringing her up" properly. This is what she said to me about her role in her daughter's school troubles.

> It was really frustrating for me. . . . I wanted her to do well like my other kids, A and B students, and then here she comes with Ds and Fs.

That weighed on me kinda bad. And maybe, I look back now, maybe in my own way I was trying to get her to do something she wasn't capable of. I don't know. Trying to get her up to an A or B from Ds, Cs, or Fs. Maybe I had some part in that . . . I don't know. But in your mind, you don't think you're doing wrong. You just trying to get them to do the best that they can and I kept thinking that she could do better. But then maybe she couldn't. I don't know. I couldn't figure that. But that was frustrating to me. To be in that kind of a predicament, you know. It was stressful. . . . I do feel like it was my fault, in some of that in bringing her up. I always felt like that. . . . I think that I failed somewhere.

If Carol Dumay felt guilty about what she had done for her daughter's schooling, she also felt guilty about what she felt she hadn't done. She told me, "I truly believe that maybe I should have started doing something before second grade." Remarkably, Michelle Phils attributed her daughter, Joy's, school problems to her "weakness" during Joy's birth. "If I'd been a stronger person [the doctors] wouldn't have had to do all those things [i.e., medical interventions] and that may have made it all better." Other moms were plagued by the general worry that "you're not doing enough for your child," as Rosa Jones put it.

Among the parents I interviewed, there was this sense that there had to be an explicit cause for their children's struggles in school. Parents did consider the consider the school's role in their children's academic problems and many mothers and fathers actively explored the possibility that their children's school troubles could be traced to a learning disability (I'll talk more about both these possibilities in Chapter 7). But, more than anything else, the mothers I spoke to blamed themselves for their children's school troubles. Mothers felt guilty over what they thought they did, what they thought they didn't do, or what they wished they could have done, as in the case of Edna Bunker who said, "I guess I just feel guilty that I can't fix it."

If mothers blamed themselves for their children's school troubles, so did some husbands. Rosa Jones said her husband accused her with the remark, "What you doin'? How come you didn't help him read?" John Cooper (in his wife's presence) suggested that his wife's "coddling" had been a factor in their son's school troubles. John Mandel shifted the responsibility for their daughter's learning problems to his wife with the remark, "It's your field." The closest any father came to blaming himself for his child's school trouble was Ralph Thorn's insight that his sons' attention deficit disorder might have genetic roots in his own childhood learning problems. This insight carried no apparent guilt, however.

School trouble, as I have documented, had a significant emotional impact on each and every family member. The burden of guilt is, among the parents I interviewed at least, a uniquely maternal response to school trouble which I find very troubling. The mothers I interviewed had made extraordinary sacrifices for their children whom they loved very deeply. Yet, in their eyes, they either hadn't done enough or had done the wrong things. Perhaps, like Elma Kinkead, they compared themselves to some ideal mother who didn't yell or scream, who didn't expect too much or too little of their children, who would have been stronger during childbirth, who would always do just the right thing at just the right time. To the extent that this is true, the cultural imposition of an "ideal mother" against whom mothers can compare their own actions is a setup which will always make mothers feel less than adequate, even under the best of circumstances. Under less than ideal circumstances, when schooling goes wrong, for example, mothers' guilt can be painful and destructive, robbing women of some of the pleasures of parenthood.

"They Treat Single Parents Differently."

Of course, not all mothers experienced the emotional and material burdens of school trouble in the same way. Individual mothers drew on various financial, community, and inner resources to cope with the challenges of a child who struggles in school, but not all mothers had access to the same resources. Some of the mothers I interviewed also felt that various forms of discrimination exacerbated the burdens of school trouble.

Betty Blake, for example, expressed her belief that she and her son were the victims of both racial and gender discrimination on the part of the education system. She was quite concerned that the school's desire to label her son as a behavior problem was related to a view of Black males as menacing and dangerous.

> As a parent, you are reading this [the school's report on her son's behavior problems] about your child. And he's a Black boy. He's a Black male in the school system. Okay? And I'm very touchy around that subject and okay, I don't know if you can understand where I'm coming from, but it's a big issue and it's a big concern for me as a single parent raising a Black boy in the system.

As it turned out, Betty Blake wasn't alone in this feeling. The construction of Black males as a problem by teachers and other school officials was an issue that was raised by several of the Black parents I interviewed. John and Marilyn Cooper, for example, worried that the attention deficit disorder (ADD) label was being used against young Black males in her community. "ADD has been on such an uprise here . . . with *our* male children," Mrs. Cooper told me.

Betty Blake also felt that the school didn't take her concerns seriously because she was a single mother. "I think that they tend, that the schools, based on my experience, is that they treat single parents differently," is how she described it to me. To protect herself from this kind of discrimination, Betty took a (male) friend of the family with her to school conferences so "they wouldn't try to intimidate me," something she believed had happened the only time she met with school staff alone.

Betty Blake struck me as a person who is always determined that no one will take advantage of her. For this reason alone, I might have dismissed her assertion that her status as a single mom had disadvantaged her in her dealings with the school if I hadn't heard similar claims from most of the single mothers with whom I spoke. Celine Street also told me that the school tried to "push her around" because she was a single mom. She compared her treatment by school officials to an incident where a man challenged her with his belief that many social problems could be traced to the "fact" that "there are too many single mothers in this world." She felt this is how the school treated her, too.

Other single mothers told me stories of principals who never returned their phone calls or school officials who "talked down to them," but the most disturbing example of discrimination against a single parent came from Molly Reeves. The school recommended that Molly's son, Steve, be promoted to third grade even though "he got straight Fs" on his report card and he was "so far behind." She was, however, reluctant to challenge the authority of the principal because "I thought whatever the principal says gotta go." But, finally, she met with the principal and told him:

> "You can't pass him. That's how I was done when I was a kid. They just kept passing me. I went to the seventh grade and couldn't read a lick." I argued with that man and he kept telling me, "Well, we got to pass him for the first quarter." Like I said, I didn't know nothin' about it, so I thought all right. He never did put him back.

It was about this time that Molly began taking Steve to a university reading clinic for tutoring. When the professor who directed the program heard about Molly's dilemma, she offered to accompany Molly to a previously scheduled appointment to help Molly plead her case with the principal. When Molly agreed, Professor Josephs called the principal's secretary to ask if this would be acceptable. Although Professor Josephs never even spoke to the principal, the principal's secretary called Molly the same day to communicate the principal's decision that he would agree to retain Steve in second grade.

This example illustrates Molly Reeves' helplessness in influencing how the school responded to her son's academic struggles. Nothing she said could move the principal from his decision to promote her son to third grade, but learning that a university professor had taken an interest in Molly's grievance, he capitulated almost immediately.

Single mothers weren't the only parents who were treated shabbily by the school system. Sophisticated mothers and fathers in two-parent families like David and Amy Thibault, Martin and Betty Springs, and Alice and John Mandel also complained about intransigent teachers and principals—particularly at the high school level—who were deaf to their concerns. I also know married women who suspect that they aren't treated as well by teachers and principals (particularly principals) when their husbands aren't present. Still, taken together, the stories I heard from single mothers suggest that the emotional burdens of having of a child who struggles in school are exacerbated by (some) school officials who do not take them or their concerns seriously. I'll talk more about this in Chapter 9.

Overall, my interviews indicate that the burdens of school trouble fall most heavily upon mothers and that marital status, race, and social class—Molly Reeves was a White, urban, Appalachian woman on welfare—can, in some cases, increase that burden. The burden of some mothers was also increased by insensitive husbands who refused to offer much "help with the children" or even blamed mothers for children's difficulties in school, and the unfortunate male tendency to minimize women's feelings (I have been guilty of this myself).

I am not claiming that fathers are unaffected by school trouble. As I made clear in the previous chapter, no family member can escape the stress of school trouble. Many of the fathers whose wives I talked to or who I talked to directly reported significant emotional stress as a result of their children's struggles in school. Many fathers also shared in the material responsibilities of supporting their children's schooling, and two fathers, David Thibault and George Connor, assumed nearly complete charge of their sons' schooling. Such fathers were rare, but it is worth noting that Amy Thibault and Catherine Connor were the only two mothers who did not express (to me, at least) any feelings of guilt over their children's struggles in school. I would not want to generalize on the basis of two cases, but the experience of these two families does suggest that fathers play a major role in the degree to which mothers feel the emotional and material burden of school trouble.

One way mothers (and fathers) tried to relieve some of the emotional stress of school trouble was by locating the *cause* of their children's difficulties. The search for labels is the topic of the next chapter.

Chapter Seven

Living with Labels
The Search for a Cause

When they got through the testing, guess what? The psychologist said to me, "Well, yes, your child is learning disabled." So at that stage my throat choked up and my eyes welled up. Well, I knew that, but it's still, when you get that label, it was still hard for me.

—Interview with
Michelle Phills

When my daughter, Anne, was in fifth and sixth grade and her school troubles were at their worst, the teachers at her school strongly *encouraged* (read: pressured) my wife and I to allow Anne to be tested for possible placement in special education. Being formally identified as a child with special needs would have made Anne eligible for individual or small group support from the special education teacher as well as special adaptations of the classroom curriculum (e.g., modified grading system, alternative assignments and exam formats, and so on). I have no doubt that these supports would have been helpful as Anne approached high school and the academic demands increased. However, based on my experience as a special education teacher and my reading of the research on the efficacy of special education, although placement in a special education program may be the best option for *many* students who struggle in school, it may not be best for *all* students for whom school is a struggle (see Allington and McGill-Franzen 1989; Glass 1983;

Parkay and Bartnick 1991; Smith 1986; Taylor 1991). Allington and McGill-Franzen (1989), for example, conclude that "the expectation that participation in remedial or special education will enhance [students'] access to larger amounts of higher quality instruction remains yet unfulfilled" (p85). I was convinced that Anne was one of those children for whom the costs of special education outweighed the benefits. Therefore, we resisted the school's efforts to *identify* Anne as a student with special needs. For her part, Anne refused to even consider the possibility of submitting herself to this process. In Anne's mind the cost of being stigmatized as "stupid" (her words) outweighed any perceived educational benefits of being labeled.

Even with the wisdom of time, I can't be certain that our refusal of even the possibility of special education for Anne was the best decision. It is impossible to know, for instance, what would have happened to Anne if she hadn't changed schools. If she had gone to the local public high school, we may have had little choice but to agree to an alternative placement. Still, the decision over whether or not to have Anne tested and (possibly) labeled created considerable turmoil in our family. So, when I interviewed parents about their experiences with their children's schooling, I was especially curious about how (or whether) they had handled the labeling issue. In general, the parents I interviewed had a range of experiences with the issue of labeling. Not all of parents I interviewed had children who had been labeled or even evaluated for possible placement in special education. But, at some level, labeling was an issue for nearly all the parents to whom I spoke.

"He's Been to a Lot of Doctors."

Edna Bunker had taken her son, Mike, to several doctors "to see what's wrong with him," as she put it. The first few doctors told her there was nothing "wrong" with her son, at least not medically. Edna, however, suspected that Mike had an attention deficit disorder (ADD) that could be treated with Ritalin. She attempted to learn more about ADD and Ritalin by attending a support group for parents of children with ADD. Edna was anxious to at least try Ritalin to see if the medication would help Mike "get organized" at school, but Mike's pediatrician was wary of Ritalin and refused to prescribe it. Perhaps as result of his reluctance to help with Mike's school problems by prescribing medication, Edna began to lose faith in the pediatrician. "I'm not thrilled with Mike's pediatrician," she told me. "I want to change him actually." Not long before I interviewed her, Edna finally found a doctor who offered her some hope. "Maybe he has ADD," he told her. "Why don't we start him on Ritalin and see how it goes?" Despite her need to find *the* cause of

Mike's school troubles and, she hoped, find a "magic bullet" for reme-
dying Mike's school problems, her son (and her husband) rejected out
of hand her desire to give Ritalin a try or to have Mike labeled ADD.
With what was for her the frightening prospect of high school looming
on the horizon, Edna was nearly desperate to locate *the* cause of her
son's problems. A trial with Ritalin was "like a last-ditch attempt" to
help her son learn to organize his schoolwork. Still, Edna worried,
"What if it doesn't work? Then what do I do?" Because of the resistance
from her son and husband she never got a chance to find out. She still
didn't know "what's wrong" nor was she at all confident she knew how
to support her son's schooling in the long term.

Other parents I met with had also invested considerable time, energy, and, in many cases, money in an effort to identify the cause of their
children's school troubles. Maria Scott, for example, recalled asking
herself, "What *is* the problem with this kid . . . who gets As in spelling
[but] reading would be a D?" At the urging of her daughter's teacher,
Maria, a single mother working in a low-paying job at a day care center and attending college at night, spent $450 for a one-hour evaluation
at the local Children's Hospital to find out if her daughter had an attention deficit disorder. Here's how she described this experience.

> Tiffany's teacher wrote down the symptoms and everything and I
> made an appointment at Children's Hospital. And we went and the
> doctor talked to Tiffany and she asked her questions about how she
> gets along with other kids, how she gets along with her teacher. . . .
> And then after the doctor got through talking to Tiffany, she talked to
> me about things that go on at home, things that I see Tiffany do. . . .
> Does she fidget or has she many friends? . . . [The doctor] told me
> Tiffany didn't have ADD. Then I said to her, "Can you tell me the prob-
> lem?" [and] she said, "Maybe she's just bored with the work that her
> teacher is giving her."

Not surprisingly, Maria didn't feel that she'd gotten much for her
money, money that she was saving to buy a house (Maria was living
with her mother at the time of our interview). Tiffany may indeed have
been "bored," but this assessment offered Maria little in the way of con-
crete suggestions for dealing with Tiffany's school troubles.

The search for *a* cause of their children's learning problems led parents like Cybil and Ralph Thorn to push the schools to test their children. The Thorns demanded that their son be tested by the school psychologist early in first grade, an unusual practice in the Megacity-area
schools where relatively few children are formally "labeled" before the
end of first grade. "They said, 'he's too young. . . . He has to be much
older before we can do any testing,'" is how Mr. Thorn recalled it. The
Thorns finally succeeded in getting their son tested by the public

schools, but it was a physician working at a child development center who they felt helped them "understand the diagnosis": a learning disability with an attention deficit disorder. This same physician prescribed Ritalin which, according to the Thorns, made such a difference in their son's behavior school that his first-grade teacher noticed the change almost immediately. For the Thorns, the formal diagnosis of their son's learning disability and attention deficit disorder made it possible for their son to qualify for special education and to be treated medically with medication.

Other parents—Diane Riggs, John Cooper, and Jeb and Janet Moore, for example—chose to have their children tested privately. Diane Riggs chose expensive private testing for her son over a free evaluation by the school psychologist so that she would have the freedom to choose a psychologist with whom she was "comfortable"—but even then she was reluctant.

> I just had him tested privately. . . . Yesterday was the last testing. I [finally] found a person I was comfortable with to test him. He's a very bright boy and I had reservations about pinpointing, setting him up as a learning disabled person.

Going through with testing her son was a significant event for Mrs. Riggs. As she told me:

> It was a big step. Like I've been asked to do it and I've received recommendations from other mothers that had problems with their children and I've put it off and off. I've made appointments to have him tested and then I've cancelled. So it's been a big step for me to find someone I'm comfortable with.

Diane Riggs worried about how a label like learning disabled might influence how people, particularly teachers, saw her son, something I talk more about in Chapter 8. But, like Edna Bunker, Diane's worries over high school overshadowed her concerns about any stigma associated with labeling. She had her son tested because she feared for his future and she hoped that identifying "the problem" would help him make the transition to high school where teachers were likely to be more demanding.

Parents took their children to psychologists, speech pathologists, and educational consultants to find the reason their children did poorly in school. Carol Dumay had her daughter's hearing tested in the hope that Georgina's reading problems might be "a physical thing." No doubt identifying a cause for their children's learning problems would have been a relief to these parents, if only because there was *a* reason. Being able to attribute school troubles to a learning disability, attention deficit disorder, or hearing loss would have eliminated more troubling explanations for children's struggles in school. If a learning disability was the cause of her daughter's problems at school, Elma Kinkead may not have worried that her "poor performance as a mother" was to blame. An identifiable cause may also have alleviated Carol Dumay's concern that she wasn't "bringing her [daughter] up properly." An attention deficit disorder or a learning disability would have provided Rosa Jones with an answer to her husband's charge the she was the cause of her son's reading problems. A label for her learning problems may have satisfied Ruth Mandel, who asked her mother, "What's wrong with me?" An explanation for his son's learning problems—in the form of a diagnosis of an attention deficit disorder—did help Ralph Thorn reshape his relationship with his son and gave him some insight into his own school experiences when he was a child as he detailed in a particularly revealing excerpt from our interview.

> It's strange and I can't really explain the first years with Al. It's a wonder that one of us didn't kill the other because everything that Al was doing was what I was, the way he was behaving and reacting was the same way I was [when I was in school] and we were so much alike, only so many years apart that we hated each other. We had a rocky relationship, fighting all the time to the point that it was physical and sometimes I just blew up in anger and he would blow up because he couldn't communicate and he would get all frustrated and I would get all frustrated and we'd start screaming at each other. It was a lousy relationship for both of us in those first years until we finally got him . . . diagnosed and I started to listen to the doctors about where his head was when he, why he was reacting the way I was. And all of a sudden everything they were saying, the problems Al was having was, yes, if that is a problem, then I had been living with that all my life.

For Ralph Thorn, identifying the cause of his son's struggles in school led to greater understanding and, ultimately, helped to transform their "rocky" relationship. "All of a sudden I started realizing the difficulties my son was having and understanding totally everything that he was feeling and the way he was behaving," he told me. His son's diagnosis also changed the way Ralph thought about this own schooling because "everything they were saying about Al" he had been living with all his life.

Gaining Access to Treatment and Services

Insight and understanding were important to parents like Ralph Thorn, but a label for their children's school troubles also raised parents' hopes that something could be done for their children. An attention deficit disorder, for example, might be treated medically with medication which, in the case of young Al Thorn, made a significant difference in his ability to cope with the demands of schooling. A learning disability, if identified, could gain access to special classes. Michelle Phills, for example, did a lot of reading about learning disabilities after she first suspected her daughter might have a "language problem," so she already "knew" her daughter Joy had a learning disability when she was given the *official* diagnosis by a school psychologist. What Michelle hoped was that the learning disability diagnosis would *require* the school to provide Joy with an education appropriate to her needs. For Joy Phills, the diagnosis of learning disability was her ticket to a *special* education. Once she was *identified*, Joy received between one and two hours per day of resource withdrawal to a special class and the support of a reading clinic (one adult and two children). When Joy entered junior high school, the school offered her full-time placement in a class for students with learning disabilities. Michelle refused this placement, however, because she felt that this class was just a dumping ground for children with a range of learning, behavioral, and emotional problems—"the garbage can of the school" is how she described it to me. Still, her access to either full- or part-time placement in a class for students with learning disabilities was contingent her being formally labeled as "learning disabled."

Even with the formal label, getting school officials to provide what Michelle believed was best educational environment for her daughter was a constant struggle. When Michelle and her daughter moved to a new school district, for example, there were few services available for students with learning disabilities and Michelle had to push hard to obtain even minimal services for her daughter ("a half an hour a day reading with six kids—a woman just reading, reading out load and having them read"). Even then, Joy had to undergo a new round of testing by the school psychologist to determine once again her eligibility for special education. Remarkably, when Joy moved back to her "old school" in Megacity, her label had more or less expired and her learning disability had to be verified by a new round of testing. Getting schools to provide what Michelle thought was best for her daughter consumed huge amounts of her time and, in this regard, she was similar to Jamie Frick and the Thorns (I'll have more to say about these parents' interactions with their children's schools in Chapter 9).

As Michelle Phills' experience indicates, the availability of services for *labeled* students varies across schools and school districts and, of course, there are also differences in the quality of these services. Michelle Phills, for example, complained that one woman who tested her child had "absolutely zero training in special education." The Thorns also complained to me about poorly trained special education teachers and inadequate programming that, in their opinion, had diminished the quality of their son's education.

Still, labels do make children eligible for services that would not otherwise be available. Dennis Street's label (attention deficit hyperactive disorder) qualified him for the services of a full-time classroom aide. Dennis' label also enabled his mother to benefit from the services of a community health nurse who made regular visits to the Street household. Celine Street credited this nurse with teaching her how to manage Dennis' behavior. Similarly, the label *language disordered* meant Diane Lau's daughter, Bonnie, could attend a special school for children with severe language problems even if Mrs. Lau, who grew up in Taiwan, didn't seem to understand either the meaning of her daughter's label or the focus of the program. A learning disability diagnosis gave Ruth Mandel access to a special resource class where she received remedial reading instruction each day. Steve Thibault, also labeled learning disabled, received the benefit of modified testing and grading procedures in his high school courses which, in his father's view, was the only way Steve could cope with the academic demands of his high school. The label *gifted* also gave Debbie Frick access to smaller, more challenging classes in which other "bright" children were enrolled.

In general, the parents I talked to were well aware of the strategic value of labeling in gaining access to certain considerations (e.g., modified testing) and services (e.g., special classes) in the schools. Tanya Wallace's daughter, Catherine, for example, attended a private school which provided no services for students with special needs. Yet, Mrs. Wallace initiated a process by which her daughter had been formally identified as learning disabled in anticipation of the day when Catherine would enter the public schools for grade 13. (In Ontario, university-bound students take a series of university qualification courses during an extra year of high school.) This is how Tanya Wallace described the process by which she hoped to have her daughter "identified."

> Catherine is going to be identified through the public school. . . . Her profiles have already gone to the psychologist. They'll do an IPRC [a meeting of school personnel at which children are formally identified as having special needs] and [if and when she transfers to the public schools] she'll get some resource withdrawal help. . . . I know she's going to need extra time to take tests and she's going to need some computer stuff.

For Tanya Wallace, the learning disability label offered her the security of knowing that, should her daughter take her university qualification courses in a public school, she would receive the extra support Tanya was sure she needed.

Like Catherine Wallace, Elma Kinkead's daughter, Andrea, was formally identified as learning disabled midway through high school, a process instigated by her mother. It didn't appear that Andrea's formal identification had led to any special adaptations in her high school courses, but her mother was looking ahead to college. Elma told me that she hoped that having Andrea identified as learning disabled would qualify her for extra support when she got to college (many colleges do offer a range of support programs for students identified as learning disabled), perhaps even easing her admission into college. Not coincidentally, Elma Kinkead and Tanya Wallace, two parents who initiated the referral of their daughters for special education in anticipation of special programs they would have access to when they attended college, had both worked as teachers in the public schools. Tanya Wallace acknowledged that accessing the "Identification, Placement, and Review" process was "pretty complicated if your child has just been in a private school." What she didn't acknowledge was her own access to the privileged knowledge that made it possible for her to navigate this "complicated" process. Other parents whose children attend private schools might not know that it is even possible to have their children identified so they can qualify for special programs if and when they enrolled in a public school or university, much less know how manage the process. I'll talk more about this kind of "cultural capital" in Chapter 10.

Alice and John Mandel also hoped that their daughter's label would improve her chances of getting a college degree. Even though Alice and John Mandel removed their daughter, Ruth, from the public school where she received daily resource support, the Mandels still took comfort in the special programs Ruth would have access to when she entered college. "To be able to go to university," Alice Mandel told me, "Ruth is going to need some adaptations and modifications. . . . She's going to need more time to do exams. She's going to need a very quiet room and that kind of thing." Without these adaptations, Alice believed that Ruth was going to have a very difficult time going to college to study drama and pursue her dream of becoming "a famous actress."

For parents whose children have been formally identified by the schools as "disabled," labels provide for access to services their children needed to survive in the public schools. Providing special programs in our schools and universities to help children and adults cope with, and possibly overcome, their disabilities is not unfair, as some conservative politicians have claimed. Children with special needs require special programs and adaptations to take full advantage of educational opportunities that others may take for granted. Still, these programs may sometimes seem unfair to those who do not have access to them. Susan Thibault, for example, was in her final year of high school. Susan worked very hard on her schoolwork, but did not do well on tests. Susan noticed, however, that *labeled* students were given extra time to complete their tests and did not have to take end-of-semester exams in a large auditorium with hundreds of other students. As a means of relieving the burden of exams, Susan referred herself for testing in the hope that she could be identified as a student with "special needs." Ultimately, it was determined that Susan was not eligible for special education. Her story is instructive, however. Many parents have children who struggle in school who do not qualify for special or remedial programs in school. Edna Bunker, for example, did all she could to support her son's schooling but, unlike Betty Blake and Ralph and Cybil Thorn, her son did not receive any of the *benefits* of special education. What could make this unfair is the possibility that a point or two on an achievement test or an intelligence test (less than the standard error of measurement) can deny students like Susan Thibault access to special programs. There may be nothing inherently unfair about the fact that some children enjoy the benefits of special programs, but it could be considered unfair that no similar programs are available for other children who struggle in school but do not qualify for special education.

In general, there are advantages that come from labels. My parent interviews indicate, for example, that insight, understanding, relief from guilt, and access to special programs and services are among the positive aspects of labeling. But there were also negative aspects of labeling that troubled many of the parents I interviewed.

"My Child Is Damaged Goods."

While parents I interviewed recognized the benefits of labels they were also, in general, painfully aware of the costs of labeling. Labels can, for example, lead to a kind of tunnel vision which fixes attention on children's "problems" while blinding teachers and parents to their achievements. Cybil Thorn, for example, initially responded to her son's learning disability label as if he had "a brain tumor or cancer or something as bad." "My God, my child is damaged goods," is how Cybil's husband described her response to the news that their son had a learning disability. It took her some time to get over her worries that a learning disability was a *life sentence* that threatened every aspect of her son's academic, social, and vocational future. "He's not going to be able to make a living. He's not going to be able to get a degree. He's not going to be able to get by in school. . . . He won't be able to function in society," is how she first saw it. Another way her son's label affected Cybil Thorn's vision, according to her husband, was that

> Cybil would always try to excuse every difficulty, every problem that Al was having, you know, "It's okay because you're learning disabled." She was labeling him more than anybody else. And Al was getting the point, "Well, I can't do this because I'm LD. And I can't get along because I'm LD and I'm different because I'm LD."

Ralph Thorn worried that the label *learning disability* affected how his wife viewed their son and how their son viewed himself. Certainly, looking at children through the lens of school troubles can affect how parents see their sons and daughters. The effect of labels on the expectations of teachers, parents, and children has long troubled educational researchers and there are studies suggesting that labels have a powerful effect on teachers' expectations which in turn can influence student achievement (see Allington 1980; McDermott 1993; Rist 1970; Smith 1980). Perhaps this is why Jamie Frick initially thought that labeling her daughter, Debbie, would be "not helpful" for her development. Concerns about the effects labels can have on the perceptions of teachers, parents, and classmates may have been the reason Mike Bunker and Archie Moore resisted their parents' efforts to have them labeled. Like my daughter, Anne, they may have worried that to be labeled is to be thought "stupid." (The effect of labels on the perceptions of parents and teachers is something I'll take up in more detail in Chapter 8.)

It was an entirely different issue that troubled Betty Blake and John and Marilyn Cooper about the use of labels. These parents worried that labels were being used as part of a larger process of pathologizing the behavior of young Black males. Betty Blake, for example, shared with me her suspicion that race was a factor in the school's efforts to label her son, an eight-year-old "Black boy," as a "behavior problem" (see Chapter 6). Similar concerns were behind Marilyn Cooper's perceptions about the number of young Black males for whom Ritalin was being prescribed in her town.

> It seems like it's been quadrupling and a lot of *our* young children are on this Ritalin. Maybe some need to be on it, most of it is just behavior problems or because of the breakdown in the family structure. Or they're not noticing the different weaknesses of the children and working on that. That has been a sad thing for me to look at and how many Black boys are on this medication. . . . ADD has been on such an uprise here in Midtown with *our* male children.

Some of the parents I interviewed recognized the costs of labeling, but concluded that, in the end, the benefits—that is, access to special programs and program modifications—outweighed the costs of labeling their children. Other parents reached the opposite conclusion: Whatever the benefits of labeling, the costs—including the negative effect of labels on people's expectations—were just too high. The Coopers, for example, rejected the school's efforts to label their son by removing him from the public school in favor of homeschooling. This was despite the financial burden that this placed on their family. The *benefits* of special education were also insuffient for the McIsaacs to keep their sons in the public schools. Their older son had already been identified as learning disabled and when their younger son's teacher mentioned something about possibly, somewhere down the line, a learning disability. . . . When she said that I thought, this child, no way! Whatever is happening, there's no way. I thought I should stop it right now. And Colin came out.

Like the Coopers, for the McIssacs the burdens of home schooling were outweighed by the cost of having another son labeled. Nor were adaptations and special programs enough for the Mandels to keep their daughter in the public schools. At the end of eighth grade they transferred their daughter, Ruth, to an expensive private school that they believed would be more congenial to Ruth's abilities.

Parents made it clear that labels led to insight, understanding, and services. But this wasn't enough for the Wallaces, McIsaacs, Mandels, or Coopers who, like my wife and I, felt that the costs of special education, at least for our children, were too high. Still, these families had the material resources that enabled them to make other choices. Michelle Phills, on the other hand, told me that she would have loved to have been able to put her daughter in a private school, but she just "couldn't afford it." The Moores, the Riggses, and the Thibaults reluctantly agreed to special education for their children, in part, because the alternatives were either too expensive or too inconvenient. For these parents, and many others I'm sure, labels were, above all else, a means of securing the services their sons and daughters needed to survive in the public schools. From this perspective, the need for labels is as much a function of the structure of schools as it is the (dis)abilities of the children they serve (Skrtic 1991).

Chapter Eight

Looking at Children Through the Lens of School Troubles

I grew up in a home where your academic performance was the most important thing. I mean my parents were both teachers and it wasn't enough that you did well. If you came second in the class, that wasn't good enough. If you had 98 percent, well what happened . . . It wasn't abusive, it was that the expectation was that I would excel. I grew up valuing the ability to do well in school. . . . I remember before I had Catherine, talking about a boy or girl or tall or short or whatever, and I remember very clearly saying, "As long as they're smart!" That was the most important thing.

—Interview with
Tanya Wallace

Not long after I interviewed David and Amy Thibault, David called me to express his disappointment that our conversation had focused so much on what his son Steve did poorly—that is, school. "We never talked about how funny Steve is," he said, "or how popular he is with the other kids in his class. All we talked about was how bad he does in school." Other parents I interviewed also found that fixing their attention on school trouble made it easy to forget how funny, popular, bright, and talented their children were. Robert McIsaac's skill on the soccer pitch, for example, was overshadowed by his "grade two reading level." Ruth Mandel's acting ability could not overcome her difficulties with "the processing of information." Sam Springs' formidable presence on the hockey rink did not make up for the fact that he'd "been slow to start in terms of literacy—reading and writing" and continued to struggle academically even in high school. In a school program in which art was barely an afterthought, Joy Phills' artistic talent did not compensate for problems with "visual-spatial abilities." Max Connor was so skilled at "getting out of mazes" that he "beat two master's students and a college freshman at a maze contest." Still, this was small consolation for the fact that he "has a lot of problems with reading . . . and he can't spell very well." Nor did the award Archie Moore won at the state fair even begin to offset the effects of being "miserable for six and a half hours a day."

Still, the parents of Archie, Max, Joy, Robert, and Ruth thought to tell me something about their children's abilities within a larger discussion about their *dis*abilities, what they could not—or did not—do well. Other parents, like David Thibault, forgot to say much at all about their children's talents and abilities. To be fair, the focus of our interviews was *school trouble* although this didn't stop some parents from at least mentioning their children's strengths. But, given my own experience with my daughter, Anne's, struggles in school, I know how difficult it is to remember that all children, no matter how mightily they struggle to do well in school, are bright, capable people. All humans, except for the most seriously handicapped, are remarkable for their intellectual, linguistic, creative, and physical abilities. But it's easy for parents (and teachers) to lose sight of this fact when they are overwhelmed with the various demands of school troubles.

Schooling is important in our culture, linked to a range of social and vocational rewards. Many homes are like Tanya Wallace's, where "academic performance was the most important thing." All the parents I interviewed had aspirations for their children. Elma Kinkead, for example, took it for granted that her daughter would go to college, but worried "about whether [her daughter's grades] are going to be good enough to get her into university . . . 'cause the competition is stiff." Molly Reeves, on the other hand, hoped that her sons would learn to read well enough to get a "good-paying job." Whether their aspirations were for their daughters and sons to go to graduate school, get a bachelor's degree, graduate from high school, or just learn to read, the parents I interviewed generally believed that success in school would make a significant difference in their children's lives. David Thibault offered a particularly thoughtful analysis on our culture's faith in the value of schooling.

It makes a tremendous difference if your kid is performing at the level of enhanced and enriched and gifted. The perception is that for those kids the future is bright and that they will be the ones who will excel and have good jobs and live happy lives and have good marriages and good relations with their kids and cook well—that everything will come to those who perform well in school. And then there's the "general level" kids whose futures are tentative [and] "basic level" kids for whom the future is threatening because whatever it is, their poor performance in school is going to condemn them to a life of marginal existence in the economy, that they will only be able to hang out with others like themselves. You're talking about peer groups and things like that, that their friends will have the same low performance and low expectations and low life chances and that they will marry people who have that same. . . . You can create this whole nightmare scenario that follows along with a kid's poor performance in school. And so, you wonder and you worry, you say, "Where is my kid relative to these other kids?"

Living in a rural, working-class community, the Thibaults had plenty of evidence that people live happy, fulfilled lives without the benefit of a college education. As David Thibault pointed out, secretaries and checkout clerks at the grocery store, for example, lead lives every bit as satisfying as many doctors and lawyers (and there are plenty of highly educated people who live lives that are neither happy nor fulfilled). In general, the correlation between status, income, and happiness is uncertain. Still, it isn't easy to resist cultural imperatives about the necessity of higher education. Martin and Betty Springs, for example, tried to downplay the necessity of going to college. "We used to talk [to Sam] about not everybody having to go to university," Mrs. Springs told me. Mr. Springs rationalized it this way:

We've told our kids, you don't have to be a great wizard. There are people out there who have to be mechanics. And they're doing fine. And in some cases a plumber may make even more than an educator. Anything like that. If you are looking at money-wise or anything. . . . Let's just take it one year at a time, we told them. Don't worry about university. Don't worry about college. I guess we've all been raised on the principle that you go to high school. You go to college, university. All this allows you to get a great job, get money, and you live happily ever after. It's not necessarily true. In certain cases it works out very well for quite a few. In other cases maybe it doesn't. I think what we've found out is that there are a lot of kids growing up around here, a lot start university or start college and then just drop out. And now they aren't doing anything in some cases. And other ones are doing very, very well. . . . As long as you're happy. You can drive in an old clunker. You can have a rented house. You can be living somewhere in a trailer if you want or bunking somewhere, as long as you're happy.

These are, I think, admirable sentiments but, as our interview made clear, the Springs' children received contradictory messages when it came to the imperatives of higher education. Yes, Betty and Martin Springs told their son that there were worthy alternatives to college, but, as Betty Springs observed, "our kids are used to the good life. There are certain things they've come to expect." These "certain things" may be difficult to obtain, however, without the high-paying jobs that frequently require a college education. It may be OK to be a handyman or an assembly line worker, but Sam and his family probably don't even know people who have these kinds of jobs. It may be possible to be happy "living somewhere in a trailer," but all the happy people the Springs know all live in "nice" houses with two-car garages and large yards. As Betty herself pointed out,

> Part of the pressure on Sam is the family he lives in. Among the personal friends we have university is just kind of a given. And for Sam, he's not too sure that's for him. And I have to say for me, I want him to do that [go to college]. And if that's something that isn't . . . if the options are taken away from him, given his secondary school performance, that's a worry.

Certainly, it isn't easy to put schooling into a reasoned perspective given the taken-for-granted relationship between school achievement and life success in the popular imagination. The priorities of schooling account, I think, for the effect of school troubles on the way some of the parents I interviewed became adept at using the language of school trouble to talk about—and understand—their children. Viewing her daughter through the lens of school trouble, Alice Mandel was able to use educational jargon quite skillfully to describe her daughter's strengths and weaknesses.

> The diagnosis is a visual-spatial problem, but I think it goes further than that. The problem seems to be the processing of information at the very highest level . . . where she has to pull things together, or analyze them, synthesize them, get them down in a logical, coherent fashion and organize it. She does well in terms of punctuation, grammar, spelling, you know, all that kind of thing. . . . Her spelling is way up, in the 80th percentile. But when she writes spontaneously, the spelling just goes. If you were to give her a grammar test, she would do really well. But when she writes, it's just that pulling it all together. So maybe it's a nonverbal disability that affects the verbal, written, it's really written and verbal. It involves so much organization and the need for constant self-monitoring and self-evaluation. On the other hand, she has real strengths that don't really fit because the metalinguistic skills have always been outstanding and she has a really good visual memory. And yet that didn't seem to help her to read. She

struggled to learn to read. So all the literature that says that phono-logical segmentation should help her learn to read, but it didn't.

Alice was, perhaps, the parent most fluent in the jargon of special and remedial education, but she wasn't the only parent who used the language of schooling to make sense of her child's school trouble. Other parents invoked special education codes like attention deficit disorder (ADD), learning disabilities, and language problems when they talked about their children. Many parents were also able to provide precise estimates of their children's reading levels and achievement test scores and discuss the contents of their children's Individual Education Plans (IEPs).

Language is a means of communicating our understandings of the world we inhabit. The language of special education, for example, can be employed to provide more precise descriptions and understanding of children's school performance. However, language, by focusing on particular aspects of our environment, can also have the effect of shap-ing understandings (Gee 1990). For example, the language of special education—emerging within a medical model with its emphasis on *ab*-normality and *dis*ability—constructs a lens for viewing school trouble that fixes attention on what's wrong with the child (McDermott 1993). The language of special education makes it more difficult to consider either children's talents and abilities or alternative explanations for children's school trouble that implicate, for example, narrowly focused, overly-prescriptive curricula; tedious lessons; sterile, institutional envi-ronment; indifferent teachers; or, school policies that treat students like inmates. As I will discuss shortly, parents can, and often do, resist these understandings, but it requires some effort to reject the framework im-plicit in the language of special and remedial education.

"It's Too Good to be Yours."

What I find is that teachers, they have in their minds a concept of how a child should act in class and if the child sways from the mold or whatever it is, the ideal child they have in their mind, then there is something wrong with that child.

—Interview with Betty Blake

Sara Lawrence Lightfoot (1978) observed that teachers' perceptions of individual children become fixed over time. She says:

Rather than teachers gaining a more in-depth and holistic under-standing of the child, with the passage of time teachers' perceptions become increasingly stereotyped and children become hardened cari-catures of an initial discriminatory vision. (86)

When Sam Springs—with some general guidance from his mother—produced an excellent essay for a high school science project, it received a failing grade. "It's too good to be yours," is what his teacher told him (see Chapter 4). Viewed through the lens of school trouble, Sam was seen to be incapable of producing good work.

Many of the parents I interviewed complained that teachers had difficulty going beyond their vision of (some) children as "problems." Jeb Moore, for example, expressed his disappointment that Archie's second grade teacher had him "labeled before he even got to her class." He attributed this to the tendency of teachers to "you know, talk between themselves. . . ." Edna Bunker attributed her son, Mike's, failure to make his school's soccer team to his reputation among the teachers at school: "You get a name for yourself and people don't want to be around you." And Sam Springs' parents were convinced that his teachers' responses to him and his work was influenced, at least in part, by his nonconformist "skater" attire.[1] Sam's math teacher opened a five-minute parent conference with her observation that:

> "You know, I'm really concerned about his pants. . . . I've seen his underwear you know. . . . To which Mrs. Springs responded: "You know what? It drives us crazy too. [But] you have pick your battles. We've decided that's not one we're going [to fight]. But we are concerned about his math. . . ."

In general, parents were frustrated by the tendency of schools and teachers to fix their attention on the negative—that is, what students did not do well. Mrs. McIsaac spoke for many of the parents I interviewed when she told me:

> That was another very sad thing at school. Even when he went to get the special ed . . . they could only just give you, see the bright side of him. It always seemed like "we have a long way to go" [or] "he's at a grade two reading level." You never got any sense of hope. I think that broke me down. They never say, "Well, he's a very bright. . . ." It was always something negative. It was like I could see something that no one else could see. Maybe the educators could see that, but they didn't put that forth. It was always, "Well—" They couldn't guarantee that [the remediation] was going to work, this grade two year, grade three year . . . whatever. We didn't expect a guarantee, it would be nice to have a sense of, that they could see the spark that you could see. I don't think any of them could see that.

A similar gaze by her son's teachers also weighed heavily on Betty Blake.

---

[1] In the event that fashions have changed since the writing of this book or if readers aren't aware of styles of dress among teenagers, "skaters" (or skateboarders) wear their pants low, which is how his math teacher could "see his underwear."

Timmy's teachers still haven't said anything about the fact that he's excelling academically. [They're] only focusing on his behavior [problems]. They still have not said to me, 'cause nothing had been wrong academically with him. He's not failing. So they can't come to me academically, behavior. And they want his behavior addressed.

Betty Blake and Sheila McIsaac wanted desperately for the schools to see beyond the negative to see what they could see: that their children were highly competent people who, like all children, possessed some extraordinary skills. But, like John Cooper, they found it "a frustrating thing when you as a parent know what the capabilities of your child are."

Betty Blake had an additional concern about the school's perception of her son: that the school's construction of her son, Timmy, was affected by race. Betty Blake didn't dispute how the school described Timmy's behavior at school. She did, however, dispute the significance of his behavior. For example, early in second grade Timmy received an "in-school suspension" for his role in a fight on the playground. To quote from the letter from the school as Ms. Blake read it to me: "This letter is to inform you that Timmy Blake is serving ['Like he's an inmate,' Betty interjected] a half day in-school suspension for physical assault." Again, Betty Blake was concerned about how schools constructed young, Black males (see Chapter 7). For the school to use the language of the penal ("serve") and judicial systems ("physical assault") to describe the actions of a seven-year-old boy is troubling, especially when that boy happens to be one of the few Black males in his school. Betty Blake is not alone in her concern that race affects how schools *see* children. A Black parent interviewed by Lareau (1992) had a similar perception:

> I've heard that some young black boys are maybe singled out more often for discipline than young white boys and maybe put one of the black boys on detention a lot faster than one of the white boys who maybe do the same things. I haven't seen it but I've heard people talk about it that work there that ought to know. (13)

Race was an issue raised by most of the Black parents I interviewed when they talked about their relations with their children's schools.

"That's Not Valued in Schools."

On the one hand, the parents I interviewed allowed their vision of their children to be influenced by the language of school trouble. Yet, most of these same parents also hoped that schools would—or even could— acknowledge that there was more to their children than *school trouble*.

Betty Springs, for example, wished that the schools could recognize Sam's natural athleticism, but "that's not valued in [Canadian] schools," is how she put it. Sam was a star hockey player. He'd been "on water skis [and] snow skiing since he was about four years old." He "skateboards [and] handles that jet boat out there . . . drives a motorcycle. . . . He'll read a hockey book. He'll read a motorcycle book. [But] these things are not in the curriculum," Sam's dad told me.

Sheila and Walter McIsaac would have liked their son's teachers to have noticed that Robert was "very advanced in his assessment of people and . . . a very instinctive kind of child. He, like, he can see through situations. He can see through things. . . . He's very perceptive." Catherine Connor would have been so pleased if Max's teachers could have discovered his social maturity and his skill as a builder of things. "He understands space," she told me. "He can build models. He loves to build models. He'll build anything." And Michelle Phills would have liked her daughter's teachers to find a way to accommodate the fact that Joy's "creativity is so phenomenal." But, in general, the structures of schooling—something I'll say more about in Chapter 10— did not permit school personnel to view students through the lens of strengths. In the context of schooling, Robert McIsaac, Max Connor, and Joy Phills were viewed in terms of disabilities and deficits.

Parents also wished that schools would take seriously their assessments of their children's academic abilities. As John Cooper observed, "it's such a frustrating thing when you as a parent know what the capabilities of your child are" and the school won't listen. When the school determined that Peter Cooper had a "reading problem," based largely on his performance on the school district's reading test, John Cooper wanted Peter's teachers to know that Peter

> read the Bible to me every night, little Bible stories . . . [and] he was able to answer all the questions that I would ask him. . . . He was comprehending what he was reading. [Yet] I had this teacher over here telling me that he can't read, he can't do this, he can't do that.

Similarly, Mrs. Lau, a recent immigrant who was overwhelmed by the arcane language and complex rules and regulations of special education that labeled her daughter, Bonnie, as a student with a "language problem," wished that Bonnie's teachers knew that Bonnie spoke both Mandarin and Cantonese—but not English—at home. Bonnie Lau also took piano and dance lessons during her overly-busy evenings. Mr. and Mrs. Mandel would also have liked Ruth's teachers to know that, whatever her struggles at school, Ruth was an avid reader at home. "She loves Anne Rice," they told me.

Parents are rarely offered opportunities to participate in the assessment of their children and, in general, their judgments are often dismissed as "biased." (Edwards 1999 is an exception to this tendency). Given my own experience as a classroom teacher and a frequent visitor to teacher staff rooms, I imagine that Bonnie Lau's, Robert McIsaac's, Sam Springs', Max Connnor's, Peter Cooper's, Joy Phills', and Ruth Mandel's teachers would have been skeptical of their parents' claims about their *abilities*. Certainly, parents are inclined to see their children in the best possible light. Still, I was convinced that, overwhelmingly, the parents I interviewed were fairly realistic in their assessments of their children's abilities. All the parents I interviewed were well aware of their children's limitations. I'm sure many parents would have agreed with Maria Scott's assessment of her daughter. "I don't think Tiffany's no genius. I know she's average." And parents like Susan Green who "knew" her son was "a very bright child" and "never doubted him," still acknowledged that his reading was "so bad." Parents just wanted a place for their children to *be*, a place that recognized and valued what they could do and supported them in those areas in which they struggled.

"They're Just Too Rigid in Their Structure."

Psychologist Howard Gardner, author of the popular theory of multiple intelligences, opens his book *Frames of Mind* by offering an example of the range of abilities that are valued in other cultures.

> Consider . . . the twelve-year-old male Puluwat in the Caroline Islands, who has been selected by his elders to learn how to become a master sailor. Under the tutelage of master navigators, he will learn to combine knowledge of sailing, stars, and geography so as to find his way around hundreds of islands. Consider the fifteen-year-old Iranian youth who has committed to heart the entire Koran and mastered the Arabic language. Now he is being sent to a holy city, to work closely for the next several years with an ayatollah, who will prepare him to be a teacher and religious leader. Or, consider the fourteen-year-old adolescent in Paris, who has learned how to program a computer and is beginning to compose works of music with the aid of a synthesizer. (1983, 4)

Gardner's point is that children possess abilities—sometimes extraordinary abilities—that often go unrecognized in our schools because of our society's narrow conception of intelligence and academic achievement (Gardner 1983; Miller 1993). Of course, dominant conceptions of what counts as intelligence (usually performance on an IQ test) and academic achievement privilege those students who possess these sorts of skills. At Boston College, for example, I work with students who perform very well on conventional measures of intelligence and school achievement. This is how they "earned" their admission to a selective university. However, these students are also fortunate to have attended schools that valued the abilities they possessed. Had my Boston College students attended schools that valued different sorts of skills—sailing, musical composition, or the ability to memorize the Koran, for example—they might not have been so successful. Some may have even been among the failures. This is, I think, at the heart of Howard Gardner's thesis. Human beings possess a wide range of abilities, but schools in our culture, sometimes arbitrarily, value some skills and devalue others. Arguably, schools in our society value skills mostly closely linked to vocational success, but this isn't always so clear. Educational reforms that privilege skills that can be measured by standardized tests, for example, necessarily devalue the kind of creativity and flexible problem-solving abilities that may be especially important to success in the highly technological workplace of the twenty-first century. The tendency of increasingly test-driven curricula to push art, music, creativity, and problem solving—because they are not amenable to quantification and measurement—out of the classroom is one of the most persuasive criticisms of the current obsession with standardized testing in our schools.

From the perspective of the parents of struggling students I interviewed, in general, narrow, test-driven curricula that fixed teachers' attention on children's *dis*abilities made no space for their children's *a*bilities. To the degree that children's school struggles are a function of (sometimes arbitrary) decisions by test makers and curriculum developers, school trouble is a social construction. After all, a different set of values by school officials might have put children who struggle in school in an entirely different light. Had Joy Phills, for example, attended a school in which art was taken more seriously she might have had a different relationship to school and schooling. Joy's language problems would not have been ignored (hopefully), but she would have also been valued for her remarkable artistic talents. Similarly, a school that wasn't so narrowly focused on the "basics" might have had a higher regard for Ruth Mandel's dramatic talent or Max Connor's problem-solving abilities. A school environment less focused on deficits and disabilities might also have found a way to celebrate and nurture Bonnie Lau's and Edward Ng's multilingualism instead of centering attention on their limitations with English.

Such schools do exist. Catherine Wallace, for example, attended a progressive, private school in which art, music, movement, and handwork were valued as much as math, science, and literacy. In our conversation, Mrs. Wallace recalled a girl who had once been in her daughter,

Catherine's, class who, despite what Mrs. Wallace described as "serious" academic problems, was remembered by her classmates and teachers only as a "remarkably gifted artist."

> When Catherine was in grades 1, 2, 3, 4, 5, there was a girl in her class who had serious difficulties—not to be compared with Catherine's difficulties—but who was the most beautiful artist I've ever seen. A child who could draw like that. And the kids will still talk about her and say, "Do you remember so and so? Oh she was so lucky, she could—" And their whole aspect, I don't think was that she was dyslexic. I don't think she was reading at all, but all they remember was the fact that this girl, what an artist! And I mean this was a gift. This was considered to be—not to say that the academic skills were not important because that was not the case—but there was much more, a wider horizon of abilities that were highly regarded [by the school].

In such a place, Catherine Wallace's academic "deficiencies" were seen by her teachers as part of an overall profile of strengths and weakness that made Catherine a unique and interesting person—not as a primary means of identification. Ruth Mandel's parents were also able to find for her a high school that made room for her talents which, no doubt, affected the way her teachers viewed her and, perhaps, how she viewed herself.

Schools that aren't so "rigid in their structure," as Mrs. Springs put it, might also have better accommodated the breadth of Archie Moore's interests, Dennis Street's energy, Debbie Frick's individuality, or Steve Thibault's humor and affability. School curricula based on the assumption that all children need to do the same things, at the same time, and in the same way will never be congenial to the wide range of abilities present in any group of students. What my colleague Carol Anne Wien calls the "train curriculum," delivering a limited array of curricular experiences in preconceived ways and prespecified times (Wien and Dudley-Marling, 1998), will always leave behind significant numbers of students. Sheila McIsaac believed that her son's difficulties in school were largely "developmental" for which the "train curriculum" makes no allowances. Betty Blake put it well:

> He's Timmy, she's Susan, and he's Tom. They are all individuals and you have to treat them as such. You can not expect them to be at the same place at the same time. It's not going to work. And my thing is that if that's what you are expecting, you are going to run into problems because you are going to get frustrated with that child.

It is widely accepted in our society that there is a wide age range in which children will begin to walk, talk, skip, ride a bike, and so on. Reflecting the "train curriculum," children who don't learn to read, write, and do arithmetic in the first year or two of school may be identified as "problems." (It is now possible for children to be referred for remedial reading help early in first grade or even in kindergarten.) Schools "too rigid in their structure," either unable or unwilling to take a developmental view, will almost certainly cause many students to be "miserable for six and a half hours a day."

There are, of course, teachers and schools that have a broad curricular focus and are able to accommodate a wide range of student needs and abilities. Sometimes these kinds of programs are available within public school settings. All of the parents I interviewed referred to one or more teachers who had created classroom environments considerate of their children's needs and abilities; for example, Debbie Frick was finally enrolled in an alternative school within her local school district. However, more common were parents like the Wallaces and the Mandels who turned to expensive private schools in order to find school curricula congenial their children's specific talents, and the Coopers and McIsaacs who decided to create an optimal learning environment for their children by homeschooling them. These options were, however, unavailable to most of the parents I interviewed who either lacked the flexibility or the economic resources to pursue either private schools or homeschooling. These are equity issues I'll say more about in Chapter 10.

Looking at children through the lens of school trouble may lead many parents and teachers to fix their attention on "what's wrong," overlooking the range of strengths and abilities all children possess. Many parents resented this focus on their children's *problems* and longed for schools and teachers that could celebrate and nurture what their children did well, although a few parents stressed that they didn't want teachers to lose track of their children's "disabilities" either.

Struggles over perceptions of children's abilities and disabilities were among the factors that complicated the relationships between parents and schools, which is the subject of the next chapter.

Chapter Nine

Parents' Relations with Their Children's Schools

You know, he's gone to special teachers for help, people have worked with him after school. I feel like he's been through everything, but no one has the same interest as I do.

—Interview with Edna Bunker

It's become conventional wisdom that there is a positive relationship between *parent involvement* and children's success in school (Edwards 1999). A number of educational researchers, for example, maintain that parent involvement is linked to high levels of school achievement, particularly in reading (Green 1995; Lareau 1989; Stevenson and Baker 1987), and it is not uncommon for educators to implicate parents when children fail in school (Valdes 1996). In Massachusetts, for example, the Commissioner of Education recently blamed parents for disappointing results on state-wide achievement tests. Based on a presumed relationship between parent involvement and educational achievement, local efforts to improve the quality of education often target parent involvement. In some communities, media campaigns have been used in an effort to get parents to attend teacher conferences, to spend more time reading with their children, or to set aside more time to help children with their homework. Other programs seek to improve the parenting skills of some (usually poor and minority) parents as a means of involving them in their children's schooling (Valdes 1996). A belief in the power of home-school relations is no doubt why parent involvement is a key component of most versions of educational reform (see U.S. Department of Education 1987).

The meaning of *parent involvement* isn't always so clear, however. Occasionally, parent involvement includes an active role for parents in decision making in their local schools. In some jurisdictions parent councils share responsibility with teachers and principals for hiring decisions and curriculum planning. In other schools, parents may not participate in decision making, but are regularly welcomed into classrooms to observe or to help with lessons. In such an environment, teachers may use parents as a resource for developing curricular units or as a source of information about children's learning needs and abilities.

Schools and teachers who welcome parents as trusted partners may be the exception, however, as many teachers prefer a professional relationship in which parents and children are positioned as clients.

> In this relationship, teachers view education as a round-the-clock experience in which parents can, and should, play a role in supplementing the classroom experience by preparing children for school, reinforcing the curriculum, and showing support (often symbolic) by attending school events. (Lareau 1989, 35)

This narrowly defined view of parent involvement "emphasizes the importance of parents being positive and supportive and deferring to teachers' definitions of children's educational needs" (Lareau 1992, 6). It is within this tradition that parents who do not (or cannot) attend parent-teacher conferences or other school events, for example, are criticized for not being sufficiently supportive of their children's education.

The parents I interviewed differed both in terms of the kinds of relationships they desired with their children's schools and in their ability to negotiate these relationships with their children's teachers. They tended to have in common, however, generally tense relationships with their children's schools. In this chapter, I consider the ways the parents I talked to were involved in their children's schooling and some of the factors that affected their relations with school personnel.

"They Don't Care. They Don't Care."

Sociologist Sara Lawrence Lightfoot (1978) commented on what she considers to be "a great irony" of schooling: "namely, that families and schools are engaged in a complementary sociocultural task and yet they find themselves in great conflict with one another" (20). Lightfoot speculates that the source of this conflict may be that "children in the family are treated as special persons, but pupils in schools are necessarily treated as members of categories" (22)—that is, not *special*.

The parents I interviewed generally acknowledged the institutional constraints on teachers, especially the limitations imposed by overly-large class sizes. I imagine that the parents I spoke to would agree with Edna Bunker's assessment that "no one has the same interest that I do"; therefore, no teacher can be expected to have the same levels of concern and commitment to the needs and interests of individual children as their parents have. No child can be as special to a teacher as they are to a parent no matter how caring the teacher. Yet, many of the parents I interviewed were content only when teachers were somehow able to acknowledge their children's *specialness*. And, for these parents, various forms of parent *involvement* were a means of achieving some degree of *special* status for their children. But, as I will attempt to show in this chapter, different expectations about the meaning of *parent involvement* can be a source of tension between parents and their children's teachers.

"The Teacher Isn't Interested Enough."

Edna Bunker acknowledged that "there is no way that a teacher can give the attention that they need to give to someone who is having problems . . . [because] classrooms are definitely too big. Way too big." But of all of Mike's teachers, it was his fourth-grade teacher who stood out for Mrs. Bunker. "She was probably his best teacher. . . . She was the one who seemed to care the most. . . . She used to send home notes saying, 'I know you can do it, Mike.'" From Edna Bunker's perspective, Mike's fourth-grade teacher treated him as if he were *special*.

Mr. and Mrs. McIsaac also had warm feelings for the teachers who were able to offer their son the individualized attention they believed he required. "Robert need[ed] a lot of individual attention, a lot of one-on-one," Mrs. McIsaac told me. But she believed that only Mrs. Bean, a special education teacher, had been able to give him the "very close attention" he needed. Had all of Robert's teachers been able to offer him the same level of *special* attention, the McIsaacs may not have chosen to homeschool their children.

Michelle Phills also had good feelings about teachers who managed to establish a special relationship with her daughter. She recalled, for example, the first-grade teacher who "understood" her daughter.

> [This teacher] totally took Joy in, she raised her as a being, she was really wonderful and she was really, really affectionate. The children loved her. She would show up in the morning and the children, they would all run at her and they would all try to hang on to her body. . . .

I still feel that Mrs. Thome set the tone for Joy's education. She really
understood her. She went for what was good about Joy.

For Michelle Phills, "understanding" meant caring for her daughter as
an individual, something she felt most of Joy's teachers had been unable to do.

Many of the parents I talked to also singled out teachers who treated
their daughters and sons with respect and affection. But Edna Bunker
and Michelle Phills were also among the parents who hoped that teachers would go beyond treating their children with "respect and affection" and recognize and support their children's *special* abilities. David
Thibault, for example, had high regard for his daughter's fourth grade
teacher who, even in an overcrowded class of forty students, found a
way to nurture her artistic talent. Tanya Wallace spoke at length about
the teachers at her daughter's private high school who were able to
recognize Catherine's strengths and weaknesses. Jamie Frick devoted
significant amounts of her time trying to find teachers who would nurture her daughter's creative and intellectual abilities (I'll say more about
this shortly). Celine Street and Cybil and Ralph Thorn also expected
teachers to recognize their children's "special needs" (i.e., attention
deficit disorder and learning disabilities), but, in order to provide an
appropriate education for their children, they felt that teachers had to be
knowledgeable about special needs. Celine told me that Dennis had
one of his best years when he moved to a school where the teachers
"were educated." These teachers understood Dennis' needs and provided the support he needed.

In the experience of these parents, such teachers were fairly rare.
The Thorns, for example, expressed their disappointment that "over
the years, we've run into very few educators, very few teachers at any
level who have any degree of knowledge or understanding about special needs." But Mr. Thorn noted that

> there were certain teachers who I got along with extremely well
> *because* they understood there was a problem. They understood that
> there was a special need. And they worked with it. If it hadn't been for
> his third-grade teacher, my eldest son wouldn't be where he is today.
> Just because of who that teacher was. He was very sensitive to Al . . .
> [to] all the kids. He'd spend a great deal of time with every child. . . .
> He'd pull their creative sides out. . . . Thank God for him.

The Thorns also singled out Al's fourth-grade teacher who, like his
third-grade teacher, "understood" their son's special needs and abilities.
These teachers were unlike Al's fifth-grade teacher who, in the Thorns'
opinion, "refused to accept" Al's special needs. This was the teacher
who, during a parent-teacher conference, "tore this kid to shreds." In

his eyes, "Al was [just] a troublemaker: He didn't work hard enough. He didn't listen. He didn't get his homework done. He didn't take notes." The fifth-grade teacher was one of many of their sons' teachers whom Mr. and Mrs. Thorn believed were unwilling or, perhaps, unable (i.e., not sufficiently knowledgeable) to provide their children with an appropriate education—that is, an education congenial to their needs as learners. And like Jamie Frick, Edna Bunker, Betty Blake, and Michelle Phills, among others, the Thorns responded to educators who failed to recognize their children's special needs and abilities by taking on the role of their children's advocates. Other parents, like the Mandels, the McIsaacs, and the Coopers, might flee from the public schools in search of more supportive settings for their children, but these parents either demanded that public school officials do whatever was necessary to accommodate their children's needs or these parents took it upon themselves to locate the best programs for their children within the public schools.

"If You Sit Back and Keep Silent, Nothing Happens."

Cybil and Ralph Thorn expected their sons' teachers to accommodate their children's special needs, which they believed was linked to teachers' "knowledge" and "understanding" of special education. But, again, in their experience, they had encountered few educators knowledgeable about special needs. The Thorns were not willing, however, to accept passively a status quo which was not, in their opinion, considerate of Al's and Ted's *special* needs as learners. As Ralph Thorn put it: "If you sit back and keep silent, nothing happens." And, by all indications, *sitting back and keeping silent* was not the Thorns' style. Here's how Cybil Thorn put it.

> We get involved with every school that our kids are involved in. We get on the PTA. We try to talk to people. We try to keep it as friendly as possible. But there comes a point when you have to see that some of the things the school is doing to meet children's special needs aren't working and [we] have to change them.

And, if school officials resist, Mrs. Thorn told me, "I'm just going to dig in with my teeth. Drive you insane until you do something." When, for example, their oldest son, Al, approached fifth grade, the Thorns were quite concerned about the availability of appropriate programs in middle school for students with special needs. "We lobbied for over a year," Mr. Thorn told me. He went on:

> What happens after fifth grade? Where do they go after that? The board of education had absolutely no plan at that point of what to do

with "our kids" after fifth grade. They figured, well, we'll mainstream them. We'll put them into the normal flow. We blew up. We started a war with the board of education. We organized nine families and we lobbied the teachers and the principal and the school board. We lobbied the board of education. . . . We lobbied . . . a trustee [who] was also one of our parents because her son was in the same class as our son. We got a politician involved . . . trying to get continuity from the fifth-grade program. [Finally] they assured us that they were going to bring in a totally qualified teacher.

In addition to this particular lobbying effort, the Thorns regularly contacted teachers, principals, the school superintendent, school board members, and local and state politicians to complain about existing programs or to lobby for new programs or additional resources. The Thorns were also active in parent groups, including a regional association for parents of students with learning disabilities, in which Mr. Thorn was an officer at the time of our interview.

Mr. and Mrs. Thorn said that they told their sons: "You're not going to like every teacher you have. . . . Unfortunately, that's life." Perhaps, but for their part, the Thorns were unwilling to tolerate teachers, administrators, or programs that weren't considerate of their sons' *special* needs and abilities. In this regard, the Thorns were similar to Michelle Phills who expected each of her daughter, Joy's, teachers to attend to her special needs and, more importantly, to do nothing to diminish Joy's self-esteem. (Michelle attributed her brother's problems with drug and alcohol abuse to "very poor self-esteem.") Michelle didn't hesitate, for example, to request a change of first-grade classrooms for her daughter based simply on a "feeling."

We arrived the first morning for first grade and all I did was *feel* the teacher—there were six or seven parents by the classroom door and we could meet the teacher. I could feel that this was not going to work for Joy. So just on total impulse and intuition I went to the office and I said that I wanted to change classes. They gave me a lot of flack for that. "How could you [ask for a change of teachers]? You haven't met the person. You have to try it out for a month or two." I said it really didn't matter to me if they thought I was neurotic or not. I just wanted to try another [teacher], so they put Joy with another teacher.

But Michelle didn't like this teacher either.

She had a Ph.D. and she wanted to be called "doctor" by the children. She made them sit in rows and she had little pieces of paper with the alphabet on and the lines and you had to trace it and it was extremely rigid and I knew with Joy, being the kind of creative person she is, I knew she couldn't do that.

Since Michelle lived in a large school district that allowed children to attend any school in the district, if space was available, she began visiting other schools to search for the school and teacher that would be best for her daughter. She found that schools were reluctant to let her observe prospective teachers, but she wouldn't be deterred.

> You know what schools are like. They do not want you to move to a new teacher. They don't want you to have any interaction about any decision about finding the right teacher. What a ridiculous idea that you just send your kid and they're just matched up with the person.

Of course, Michelle refused to accept this "ridiculous idea" and, eventually, she found an alternative school that "let me sit in [and] really understood what I was looking for." Here she found a teacher who impressed her. "She'd been teaching for about thirty-five years. I sat in on her class and I was actually tearful . . . because she was so gentle and loving with kids. This is where I wanted Joy to be." And, as it turned out, this was the teacher who "took Joy in" and "set the tone for her education."

Michelle also talked to me about another "really great teacher" her daughter had. "Her homeroom teacher whose background was special education. . . . He was a good guy, he was very helpful and good person. She had another really fortunate year that year in as much as her teacher that year was LD himself. And he had really had a sense for her . . . he really did try . . . and he was helpful to me."

A year at a "tiny" alternative school was also good for Joy.

> There were only three teachers and I could relate to all three of the teachers. And they felt that because she could design her own program there and work at her own pace, even though they didn't have specific training for working with students with learning disabilities, that it, you know, could work out. I decided to try it. Last year was pretty good. And it was the first the first time in her life that she had really awesome grades. She could get 80, 90, 100 percent on her report card. But it was because it was her own contract and it was designed to suit her.

Michelle was able to find a few "really great teachers" for her daughter, teachers who "had a sense for her" and "understood" her. But, overall, Michelle's story was one of struggle. Teachers who diminished Joy's self-esteem, disruptive students who limited her learning opportunities, and administrators who failed to provide satisfactory support for Joy's special needs led Michelle to spend a significant amount of her time searching for the right schools and the right teachers, badgering school officials to secure appropriate special education services. At the time of our interview, Michelle was engaged in another quest, this time a search for a high school that could accommodate Joy's learning disability while nurturing her artistic talent. But, in the end, Michelle wasn't very optimistic. "Joy's just not cut out for this system," she told me. "Unless you're average the system is worth shit."

"I Was Cross with the Teachers Sometimes."

If Michelle Phills and Ralph and Cybil Thorn seemed to be engaged in endless struggles for the school, the class, the teacher, and the program that best supported their children's needs and abilities, most of the parents I interviewed limited their advocacy efforts to intervening with school officials when they felt that their daughters and sons were being treated unfairly. Martin and Betty Springs, for example, met with their son, Sam's, high school teachers after Sam was given a failing grade on an assignment because the teacher didn't believe Sam had written the paper by himself (see Chapter 4). Maria Scott complained to her daughter, Tiffany's, teacher and, eventually, attempted to get the principal to intervene when she felt that the teacher had humiliated Tiffany by asserting that "her three-year-old son could do better work than Tiffany." Similarly, Susan Green told me a story about taking a day off work "to go up to the school" to challenge a grade her son, then in second grade, had received on his report card. "When I saw the D in his math, I went up to the school immediately," she said. In the end, the teacher "wound up changing his grade because she knew I was right"— that is, her son, although he struggled with reading, was good at math.

Celine Street complained bitterly to me about a teacher who punished her attention-deficit-disordered son by denying him the opportunity to participate in class trips and, sometimes, forcing him to eat alone at lunch. "The teacher lost patience with Dennis. [She] started doing things to single him out [and] telling the class not to pay attention to him . . . And the more she did this, the worse he got." So she called Dennis' teacher at her home to share her anger. Similarly, Betty Blake engaged in a series of battles with her son's school over her desire to keep her son from being constructed as a behavior problem and to challenge disciplinary tactics that were implemented without consulting her (see Chapter 8). Molly Reeves made repeated efforts to persuade school officials not to promote her son to third grade because he couldn't read. And on and on.

Perhaps most parents have attempted to intervene on behalf of their children with teachers or other school officials at least once in a while. I recall that my father's intervention with a vice principal helped to prevent my expulsion from Cleveland St. Ignatius High School. Still, the nature of school trouble—failing grades, missed assignments, behavior problems, and so on—suggests that parents of students for whom school is a struggle may have many more occasions to engage in more frequent, intense, and negative interactions with their children's schools (Edwards 1999; Lareau 1989). "I feel that I'm always over there, sort of pleading Mike's case," is how Edna Bunker described her involvement in her son's schooling.

Some of the parents I interviewed, however, desired a sustained involvement in their children's schooling that went beyond crisis management.

"Looking Forward to Being a Part of a Learning Community"

Jamie Frick, like Michelle Phills, expended considerable time and effort at different points in her daughter, Debbie's, school career in search of schools and teachers that were congenial to Debbie's "style of learning" and reflective of Jamie's progressive educational philosophy. Jamie wanted, for example, a program that stressed "process writing" and allowed Debbie to explore her talents and interests. Jamie wanted teachers who would challenge her daughter and nurture her intelligence and creativity. When Debbie "graduated" to middle school, Jamie visited "maybe ten schools" looking for the ideal program for her daughter. Jamie was also quick to intervene on her daughter's behalf if things weren't going well in school. When, for example, her daughter was bullied by boys in first grade, Jamie demanded that the school "do something" to make Debbie feel safe. And when Debbie was not excelling in her high school math program as her mother thought she should, Jamie demanded to speak to the head of the math department. But Jamie wasn't satisfied merely finding the right school for her daughter or responding to crises. She also wanted to be involved in her daughter's education by "being a part of a learning community" that welcomed her and acknowledged what she had to offer (during her daughter's early school years Jamie was working on a Ph.D. in education). She recalled fondly a principal at one of the schools Debbie had attended who was particularly open to input from parents. This principal, Jamie said, asked

> "What can *we* do?" It was just a more open dialogue around things. The principal knew I was working on my Ph.D. [and] he was asking me questions. There was a woman doing research at [the local university] on math and how little kids learn mathematical concepts and he had her coming in and doing workshops. . . . He had someone else who was doing the process model of writing. So he had kids doing that kind of writing and inventive spelling. And Debbie was producing books every week. The world was rosy. It was wonderful. He was just very open to so many different things and I felt that he was at the

leading edge of exploring different things for himself and did that for the kids.

Jamie was equally enthusiastic about a middle school her daughter had attended.

> Forest School was a unique and wonderful experience for me as a parent because I felt that it was a community and being in a city it is difficult to establish community. So I had a community of other people to associate with. I can't say that I made really close friends, but there were people I liked, people who were like-minded. . . . We had some of the most exciting curriculum planning meetings that I have ever experienced where we would sit down with our class and the class wasn't just the kids. It really was parents, kids, and the teachers.

Jamie recalled another "wonderful" teacher—Debbie's seventh grade teacher—with whom she had "developed a rapport."

If teachers who welcomed a collaborative relationship with parents made Jamie Frick's world "rosy" and "wonderful," she frequently encountered teachers who denied her this pleasure. She recalled her disappointment with her daughter's second-grade teacher, who "didn't seem to be comfortable with parent input [or even] having parents in the classroom." In this classroom, "parents were *told* rather than asked" about important instructional decisions. Jamie felt that her efforts to be involved in her daughter's education were no longer welcomed and even actively rejected. Her written requests to establish a dialogue with Debbie's teacher—at this point Debbie was "not enjoying school"— were rejected as inappropriate by the teacher, who threatened to enlist the support of the school administration to keep Jamie at bay.

Jamie also recalled Debbie's sixth grade-teacher who, in Jamie's words, had "everybody in the class doing exactly the same [math] work at the same time." When Jamie met with this teacher to express her concern, she encountered a teacher whose resistance to Jamie's efforts to engage her on a first-name basis was, in Jamie's view, emblematic of this teacher's general unwillingness to establish any kind of partnership with parents in support of children's learning.

> I went in and had the audacity, and yet from my perspective it wasn't audacity, to call her Mary. She was very quick to call me by my last name and made it very clear [to me] that she was sitting on her side of the desk and I was to sit on the other side of the desk. She wanted that divide there. She was not willing to sit down and talk to me about Debbie and Debbie's work. There was no understanding about work, or concern about where Debbie had come from, what Debbie's style of learning was. This was her style and she was running her classroom that way.

Jamie was frustrated—perhaps even to tears—by teachers who kept her at arm's length, teachers who sat on the "other side of the desk," denying Jamie both the satisfaction of having meaningful input into her daughter's schooling as well as access to a vibrant learning community that would satisfy personal and intellectual needs. So, given the bureaucratic structure of high schools, it isn't surprising that Debbie's high school years were particularly unsatisfying for Jamie, at least initially. Debbie's high school teachers resisted, for example, Jamie's request for more informative report cards. Debbie's teachers also made it difficult for Jamie to meet with them and, when she did talk with her daughter's teachers, they were not, from Jamie's perspective, especially interested in her input. Even her effort to create a community for herself by finding a way for high school parents to come together met with resistance. When Jamie suggested a "parents' night" for parents in her daughter's class she was put off with the assertion, "This is not part of our tradition."

Perhaps even more painful to Jamie, when Debbie entered high school she didn't want her mother to be so involved in her education any more. Like many adolescents, Debbie worried that her mother's involvement in her schooling would embarrass her. Jamie's need to be involved in her daughter's life was as strong as ever, but was, increasingly, thwarted by Debbie's own need to establish independence by pushing her mother away. In the end, however, Debbie was persuaded to attend an alternative high school that was more congenial to her artistic spirit, but also encouraged parent involvement even though Jamie was aware that Debbie was "concerned that it's a place where parents can be involved. . . . She still wants to maintain a space that is her space." Still, Jamie told me that she was "looking forward to being a part of a learning community where I can share some of my skills and participate in school."

Other parents I interviewed also expressed a desire to "share their skills" in support of their children's schooling. More to the point, these parents were anxious for teachers to *listen* to what they had to say since they felt they knew their children best. Celine Street, for example, tried to share what she had learned about how best to work with her son, Dennis. By all accounts, Dennis, who had been diagnosed as attention deficit disordered, was a very difficult child to work with and, based on my limited experience with him, this was certainly true. I was, however, impressed with the way Celine Street interacted with her son. She was, I thought, remarkably calm, firm, and consistent, probably the only way to work with a child as impulsive as Dennis. Celine did not, however, feel that these skills came naturally. She credited a social worker who worked with her when Dennis was a preschooler for her ability to "manage" her son as well as years of experience living with

Dennis. Yet, Celine felt that teachers who were generally uninterested in what she had to say.

Alice Mandel, an intelligent woman with a master's degree in education, also hoped that her daughter's teachers would value her expertise. However, Alice found few teachers who were interested in tapping her expertise and felt that some teachers may have even been threatened by her. In the experience of these parents, it did seem that there are teachers "who can't deal with parents who tell them what to do with their children," as Celine Street put it.

Jamie Frick, Celine Street, and Alice Mandel were among the parents I talked to who weren't satisfied with traditional roles for supporting their children's teachers. These parents also wanted teachers to listen to what they had to say which, given their intimate knowledge of their children lives, would seem to be in the interests of parents, students, and teachers (Edwards 1999; Shockley, Michalove, and Allen 1995). Yet, more often, they found teachers who were less interested in a partnership than a professional-client relationship. From this point of view, parent *involvement* is a matter of being positive, encouraging, and supportive of teachers (Lareau 1992; Lightfoot 1978). At least one of the parents I interviewed used this traditionally supportive role as a way of achieving influence with the school on behalf of her son.

Being "Nice"

Edna Bunker said that she had good relations with her son's teachers. "Why?" I asked. "Because I'm nice," is what she told me. Not being *nice*—parents who, for example, criticize teachers' disciplinary practices, demand *special* programs or curriculum, go over teachers' heads to complain to principals, reject their roles as "clients," or in other ways are unsupportive of teachers—risks, in the minds of some parents, at least the possibility that a vengeful teacher might, consciously or unconsciously, withhold academic or emotional support from their children. I must say here that the vast majority of teachers I have met over the years—and I have met many—are good, caring people. Few teachers, I believe, would deliberately do harm to a child in their care. Still, the possibility, however remote, can give parents pause. Martin Springs, for example, described his relationship with his son's school this way: "It's a lot easier to play the game and not have to risk any kind of formal retribution." Fear of "retribution" may have influenced Martin and Betty Springs to take up their challenge to the evaluation their son Mike's assignment on the Venus's flytrap (recall that he had gotten a zero on this assignment because the teacher doubted it was his work) in fairly deferential tones despite their obvious anger. According to his mother, Sam himself worried that even this "polite" challenge by his parents might jeopardize his relationships with his teachers. Fear of retribution was also a factor in my own reluctance to complain to a school district administrator with whom I was acquainted when my daughter's fifth-grade teacher failed to live up to promises she had made to provide additional academic supports for Anne. A letter to this administrator did yield some short-term changes in this teacher's behavior toward my daughter, but I suspect that a particularly negative final report card that year was, in part, punitive. It seems that, in this case, not being *nice* created tensions that damaged my daughter's relationship with her fifth-grade teacher. These fears also discouraged the Springs from taking their case to a "higher level." For the Springs, being *nice* translated into a reluctance to challenge teachers' authority. But being *nice* can also be a conscious strategy for gaining influence with teachers and other school officials. Consider how Diane Riggs discussed her involvement in her son's school.

> I've been a great volunteer over at my children's school to support the school. . . . I really threw myself in and I joined the Home and School Committee. And I went to meetings and I volunteered in the classroom. . . . I'm an accountant so I was able to do tax returns at home. So I wasn't going out every day. So I did a lot of volunteer work. . . . Roger had such a hard time. Like, for my daughter it was very easy [but] doing the same things with Roger, I had a really hard time with him. He just did not want to learn how to read. So I refocused my volunteering into the classroom, particularly for Roger. All the way through I would help in [his] class, help the teacher out because I knew she would be having problems [with Roger]. *I wanted her on my side* so I did a lot of volunteering, going for outings, helping with the reading. They had a program for second and third grade where you'd pull the child out, all of the kids, and you [the parent volunteer] would just do reading with them. They would have individual books and you'd be doing reading with them. Check it off. I did that and I did the "computers-for-lunch" program, just to be in the school, because I felt that I needed to be there to see what was going on, making sure, that Roger was doing all right.

Volunteering in her son's school gave Diane Riggs ready access to teachers making it easy for her to monitor Roger's schoolwork. "I could, on a weekly basis or even more, touch base with the teacher. It's really casual there and when you are working over there you can hop into the classroom at lunch hour or recess and you know, say, 'How's it going?' And [Roger's teacher] will give me some feedback." If there was a problem with Roger, Mrs. Riggs would be in a good position to respond to it quickly, perhaps avoiding bigger problems. For example:

> [In] the beginning of the year Roger wouldn't bring home everything. He wouldn't tell me everything that was going on. [But] I found out

by being in the school, by popping in and finding out. . . . It's just great being over there.

Of course, there are other ways to monitor children's schoolwork that don't include volunteering in schools. But being in the school so frequently gave Diane Riggs opportunities to develop relationships that enabled her to monitor Roger's schoolwork and help to get her son's teachers and the principal on her "side," as she put it. For example, Diane told me that children who struggled in Roger's school were usually requested to withdraw from the school's language immersion program. She was, however, able to keep her son in the program. "I've really got my way," she told me. "I wasn't badgered like I know some of the other mothers were to get their kids out of French immersion." She attributed this influence to the relationship she had developed with the school principal as a direct result of volunteering in her son's school.

> The principal and I would talk once a year and he would go over what I was doing with Roger and what sort of help I was getting for him. And I felt that the principal knew me because I volunteered at the school. . . . Also I have been able to request that my child have a certain teacher. . . . I know the principal fairly well so I['d] write him a note and I['d] get my wish.

Mrs. Riggs also felt that volunteering in the school gave her access to useful information. Volunteering in the school helped her to develop a relationship with the principal, for example, that enabled her to request particular teachers for her children and, because she spent so much time in the school, she had a particularly good sense of who the best teachers were. She also gained a better sense of the community and community resources. "I knew the parents. I knew where I could get help for things. I found out what was going on extra-curricularly that my kids could get into."

So, for Diane Riggs, "being nice" had nothing to do with fear of retribution. It was part of a deliberate strategy to gain influence with the school to get what was best for her children, especially Roger who struggled in school. But, if volunteering at school is a means of gaining influence with school officials, it was an avenue that wasn't available to many of the parents I interviewed, something I'll discuss at length in Chapter 10.

"I Don't Stay to Talk to No Parent."

The parents I interviewed had a range of experiences with their children's schools. Edna Bunker frequently stopped by her son's school to find out from his teachers how he was doing. Cybil and Ralph Thorn were often engaged in conflict with their sons' schools over the provision of appropriate programming. Jamie Frick sometimes worked collaboratively with her daughter's teachers to help plan and implement challenging curriculum. Susan Green and Betty Blake often challenged school officials over what they believed was unfair treatment of their children. Other parents met with their children's teachers on "meet the teacher nights" and routinely monitored their children's homework. And, of course, Diane Riggs was a frequent volunteer in her children's school.

Arguably, the interactions these parents' had with their children's schools mirror the relationships other parents have with their children's schools. The stories I heard from these parents do suggest, however, that, as a group, parents of students who struggle in school may be more likely to find themselves in conflict with school officials. Although the parents I talked to had different expectations about the kind of interactions they desired with their children's schools, virtually every parent I interviewed talked about occasionally tense relations with school officials. In extreme cases, these tensions led the Thorns to decide to "document," in writing, all their interactions with school personnel and made Maria Scott think that "public schools are not good."

Some degree of tension between teachers and parents of students who struggle in school is not surprising. Parents of children who struggle in school are likely to harbor at least some resentment toward the institution that makes their children "miserable for six and a half hours a day." Parents of children who struggle in school may also resent the focus on their children's weaknesses, as I discussed in Chapter 8. For their part, teachers may be occasionally resentful of parents of struggling students who, as a group, make additional—and sometimes unreasonable—demands on their precious time. Based on the stories of the parents I interviewed, some teachers may also resent parents who violate the professional-client relationship that some teachers prefer. And, certainly, there are few teachers (or principals) who wouldn't resent parents who "document" their interactions as the Thorns did. Clearly, teacher-parent relationships are delicate under the best of circumstances and "school trouble" will almost certainly complicate these relations. In the view of some of the parents to whom I spoke, these delicate relations were sometimes undermined by the actions of individual teachers and principals.

One frequent complaint among these parents was "poor communication" on the part of the school. The most common examples of *poor communication* took the form of teachers who minimized children's difficulties with reassurances that "everything is fine" when the evidence indicated that everything was not fine. Betty Blake, for example, complained that her son's teachers routinely assured that he was "doing great" and then he'd get a highly negative report card. Janet Moore told a similar story.

> They'd tell me Archie's doing all right [in school]. Well, how can you be doing all right—and then, like, you know, they always put satisfactory or needs help in reading—but when you talk to his teachers . . . it's not there. He's not doing this. He's not doing that. Well, how can he be satisfactory then?

To which her husband observed: "It doesn't seem that they are being entirely honest on those reports."

John Mandel also recalled a period when his daughter wasn't completing her schoolwork and "nobody contacted us. Nobody did anything about it. They just let it go." As painful as it might be to hear, these parents clearly wanted an honest evaluation of their children's schoolwork. It's easy to understand teachers' reluctance to share bad news with parents and I'm sure no parent wants to hear this kind of news. But the parents I spoke with preferred bad news to inaccurate or misleading reports from their children's teachers.

Even more distressing to parents were school officials who, at least from the parents' point of view, refused to talk with them about their children's work at school. Maria Scott told me about her frustrations with a teacher, and then a principal, who failed to return her phone calls.

> One time the teacher said [that] she didn't have time to talk. And that just made me blow up. You have her six hours a day and you don't have time to talk to me? . . . [And] the principal was a very busy person. Every time I would call, they would tell me that she would get back to me. But she never did.

Mr. and Mrs. Springs also talked about the difficulties they had scheduling meetings with their son's teachers and Mr. and Mrs. Mandel told me that, while the special education teacher did meet with them regularly in the beginning, she finally told them that she just didn't have the time to talk to them so often.

These parents expected teachers' time, yet it didn't seem that teachers were always able to spare the time to meet with parents. Teachers she felt didn't have time to "stay and talk to no parent" caused Rosa Jones to adopt a "hostile" stance whenever she met with school officials. Unresponsive teachers made Maria Scott "feel that public schools are not good," leading her to enroll her daughter in a parochial school. To be fair, I am only presenting the perceptions of parents here. Had I talked to the teachers who interacted with these parent they would, no doubt, have told a different story. They may have told me that these parents were too demanding or complained about hostile parents who struck a litigious stance by "documenting" their interactions. They may have talked about increasing demands on teachers, an increase in the number of "needy" children (and parents) in their classes, and large class sizes. Several of the parents I interviewed acknowledged the difficulty of teachers meeting the needs of their children in the face of overly-large class sizes. Still, what I found most disturbing about parents' tales of indifference is who told them. Single mothers, among the parents I interviewed, were far more likely to describe interactions with the schools in which they had felt patronized or ignored. All but one of the seven single mothers I interviewed shared stories in which they had been treated badly by the schools (e.g., failed to return phone calls, accused of poor parenting, or generally ignored). Only one "married" mother, Rosa Jones, shared a similar story and, interestingly, she is an African American woman. Although I never specifically asked this question, several of the single mothers I spoke to asserted that they had been discriminated against because of their marital status (see Chapter 6). Celine Street, for example, looking back on her experience with a school that "wouldn't listen to me," speculated about the effect of her marital status on her relationship with her the school.

> If I had a husband or father with me, because I am a single mother, then things might have been different. . . . I felt that because of my position, being a single parent, and a woman, although the teacher was a woman, that they could push me around a bit. Especially the principal. I felt that he really didn't take me seriously.

Betty Blake felt the same way. The one time she'd met with school officials by herself "they tried to intimidate me," she said. "They said things to me and they'd worked it in such a way that they made me feel as though I had no say." Betty sought to remedy her relative powerlessness with the school by having a male friend, Charles, accompany her to all meetings at her son's school.

Single mothers weren't the only parents I spoke who felt that they'd been treated with indifference by school officials. However, the fact that this was a common experience among single mothers lends credibility to Celine Street's assertion that her marital status was a factor in her relationship with teachers and other school personnel. It seems that, for the mothers I interviewed at least, marital status is one of a host of factors that affected parents' ability to interact with teachers and principals and influence school officials to acknowledge and provide for their children's *specialness*.

I opened this chapter by citing research indicating a strong, positive relationship between children's achievement in school and their parents' involvement in their school. Within the discourse of school reform, this research is often interpreted to mean that parent involvement is an antidote to school failure or, put differently, children fail in school because their parents don't care. Leaving aside the issue of what counts as parent *involvement* (given the range of ways the parents I talked to were involved in their children's schooling) it is clear to me that *all* the parents I interviewed were involved in their children's schooling. When school is a struggle, parents may often be more involved in their children's schooling (Lareau 1989). However, even though their efforts in support of their children's schooling may have affected the degree to which their children struggled in school, the involvement of these parents did not make their children's school troubles magically disappear. In general, my examination of these parents' relationships with their children's schools provides further evidence that these parents were willing to do whatever was necessary to support their children's schooling, although they differed in terms of the material and cultural resources they were able to bring to bear in support of their children's schooling. This is the topic of the next chapter.

Chapter Ten

Parents Care

Single mother, day care worker, and full-time university student Maria Scott strained her personal financial resources to pay $450 for her daughter to be evaluated for a possible attention deficit disorder. Eventually, she assumed the additional burden of $180 a month for tuition so her daughter could attend a parochial school—a "big sacrifice," Maria told me. But she felt the sacrifice was worth it because Tiffany was able to attend a "school where she feels comfortable." Of course, Maria was only one of the many parents I interviewed who made financial sacrifices so they could obtain private testing or tutoring for their sons and daughters, send them to private schools parents believed would be more congenial to children's needs, or homeschool their children. Diane Riggs and her husband, for example, gladly spent $500 a month for tutoring when their son was in second grade. The McIsaacs had no regrets about their decision to homeschool their sons even if the demands of homeschooling, by preventing Mrs. McIsaac from entering the workforce, denied their household a second income. Homeschooling also reduced the hours Mrs. Cooper could work outside the home, postponing indefinitely the day when the Coopers would be able to buy a home of their own. School trouble had financial implications for most of the parents I interviewed, but financial sacrifice wasn't the only expression of caring among these parents.

Like Maria Scott, Diane Riggs, the Coopers, and the McIsaacs, Jeb and Janet Moore are good and caring parents. They want what is best for their children, but they aren't afraid of being strict if they believe it is in their children's long-term interests. Instilling "Christian values" in their children is important to the Moores. They hoped to teach their children that "you obey the teacher, you obey the rules. . . . Certain things are right and certain things are wrong." They didn't let their junior high school-age daughter "go to PG-13 movies" even though they knew that this restriction led some of her classmates to make fun of her. Nor did they rent R-rated movies for viewing at home. The Moores initially enrolled their two children in a Christian school because they "liked the religious aspects of it." Deeply troubled over the prospect of her son, Archie, being "miserable for six and a half hours a day," Mrs. Moore "cried over him . . . lots of times." The Moores worried about Archie's self-esteem and they searched for extracurricular activities that might boost his confidence. He wasn't good at baseball, but he was good at volleyball so Mr. Moore willingly drove his son more than twenty-five miles to Midtown, the closest city that had organized volleyball for boys. The Moores "never resented the money [they] had to spend" on the tuition for their children to attend a private school or, eventually, on private testing at $40 an hour "to find out if there's something to help," or the possibility of family counseling at $80 an hour. However, when they concluded that the heavy homework burden at the Christian school their children attended threatened their son's self-esteem, they didn't hesitate to transfer him to the local public school. Mr. and Mrs. Moore preferred a school with "religious aspects," but their son's well-being was an even higher priority for them. The Moores were also willing to accept, a least occasionally, their son's claim of "no homework" as a means of relieving the burden of school trouble for him. Simply put, the Moores cared about their children and their children's schooling.

Molly Reeves left school three weeks into seventh grade and didn't learn to read until she was thirty-five years old, but she cared deeply about her sons' schooling. She wanted her boys to do better than she had and she believed education was the key to their vocational success. "I want them to read real good," is how she put it, and she frequented garage sales and "junk stores" to find books she could afford for her sons to read. When the school insisted that her son be promoted to second and then third grade despite "straight Fs," Molly tried to persuade the principal to change his mind. If her son was passed from one grade to another without learning "to read real good" he would not be able to do well enough in school to get a "good job." Clearly unhappy with how this school had treated her sons (and her), she searched for a school better suited to their needs.

> One of the ladies I used to go to church with, her daughter's a teacher and she told me about Gold Hill School. She said it was a good school and highly recommended it. [I went] down to the board of education and I told them about Joe's having all this trouble down there and I wanted him transferred to Gold Hill School. [At first] the yellow bus would come—because we don't live in that neighborhood—and pick him up and take him all the way to Gold Hill. He rode the bus a good hour and a half just getting there.

But a change in transportation policy soon threatened this arrangement. "They're not allowed to bus them from here to Gold Hill [any-
more]. I don't know why. . . . So, in order to keep them in Gold Hill
School I moved." Moving to Gold Hill, however, required Molly to put
aside her prejudices in order to do what was best for her children. Molly
Reeves is a White, urban, Appalachian and Gold Hill is a predominantly
Black school. "There's maybe ten White kids in the whole school," she
told me. Molly insisted that she wasn't a "racial person" but she added,
"You don't mix races. You stick with your own race" even though "As
far a getting along, talking to people, the kids playing with other kids,
there's nothing wrong with that." Still, she felt isolated in her new
community "'cause I don't know anybody up there. Absolutely nobody." Moving to Gold Hill also meant that Molly now had to endure a
long bus ride each day (she was working on her GED), but she preferred this arrangement to having her sons "do that every day." I certainly wouldn't defend Molly's prejudices, but her willingness to put
aside these feelings is a measure of the depth of her commitment to her
children's education.

Michelle Phills dedicated many of her waking hours to finding services that would enable her daughter to both overcome her learning
disability and develop her creative talents. For example:

> God, when I think about the things we did. . . . For three years, until
> the end of first grade, I drove her twenty miles every day for special
> work with this lady who was getting progress with kids with learn-
> ing problems by using colored lights. She was an optometrist, this was
> an experimental program. . . . It looked like Joy was improving so
> we kept going. . . . I bundled a baby up every day and drove all the
> way out there and all the way back so the stress in our lives, which
> is unbelievable, trying to keep up this thing plus fighting the school
> continuously.

Later Michelle arranged to have her daughter tested and tutored at
the local Children's Hospital. She also managed to enter Joy in a special
tutoring program at a nearby university after being "turned down five
or six times." "I called everybody I could," she told me, "and connec-
tions that I could [make] and I tried to understand how to get access to
more services—what is available and what isn't." And, when she concluded that her daughter's needs would never be adequately served in
the rural community they'd moved to, Michelle and her daughter returned to expensive Megacity. Michelle Phills did all that she could to
find the best programs for her daughter because, more than anything
in the world, she cared about her daughter's education and self-esteem.
Of course, many other parents would not have been able to spend so
much time locating resources for their children.

The parents I interviewed were a diverse group. Some were religious, some were not, and among the religious were Christians and Jews. Some were rich and some were poor although most were "middle-class." A few parents did not finish high school and several had graduate degrees. The parents I interviewed included Blacks, Whites, and Asians. I talked to husbands and wives and single mothers. My sample included both liberals and conservatives. Some were shy and reserved, others were bold and assertive. I met parents who were angry and bitter and parents who were resigned to their children's struggles in school. There were also significant differences in how the parents I interviewed responded to school trouble. Some, like Michelle Phills and the Thorns, fought tooth and nail for what they believed were the most appropriate services in the public schools for their children. Maria Scott, the Wallaces, and the Mandels opted for private schools. The Moores moved their son out of a private Christian school to a public school for the same reason. The Thibaults and the Bunkers were resigned to making the best of a bad situation. The Coopers, McIsaacs—and, for a time, Michelle Phills—took the extraordinary step of home-schooling their children. Millie Lau chose to supplement the work of the school by doing hours and hours of "mom's homework" with her "language impaired" daughter, Bonnie. Despite all these differences, every parent I interviewed had one thing in common: They loved their children very much and they were prepared to do whatever they could to support their children's education although they differed in terms of the resources they were able to bring to bear in support of their children's schooling (something I say more about shortly). These parents all cared about their children and their children's education, even if their expressions of caring may not always have been intelligible to their children's teachers.

Going "Fishin'"

From the viewpoint of many—perhaps even most—teachers, *caring* parents are those who express their support for their children's education by attending parent-teacher conferences, reading to their children every night, monitoring their children's homework and, when necessary, helping them with their school work, and generally instilling in children the values (persistence, dedication, love of learning, and so on) needed to do well in school (Lareau 1992). What then would teachers make of Mr. and Mrs. Cooper who told me:

> [Sometimes] my son needs a break. . . . He felt good that his dad was
> in his corner. From his standpoint, "Hey, my dad thinks I need a break.

> He's the head of the household and you got to listen to him." Me telling him, "Go do whatever you want to do. Take him out, get him ice cream, whatever, you know." We would take him out [of school] and do different things. Sometimes we would take him out of school and take him fishin'.

Other parents I talked to also tried to do what they could to reduce the stresses of school troubles on their children's lives. Recall, for example, the Moores who sometimes accepted their son's claim that he had "no homework" even though they knew better and how they failed to deliver on their threat to drive Archie back to school to pick up forgotten assignments, preferring not to "make matters worse" in their household. David Thibault also told me that there are days when he feels that homework isn't so important. "Go down the hill. Go down to the river. Go play with your friends. Go ride your bike. . . . Enough of schooling. There's more to life" [than school].

Betty and Martin Springs were also attempting to put their son Sam's schooling into a more reasoned perspective.

> We've done a lot of talking this summer. We're building him up and I guess what we've decided to do is just to take the pressure off [him] totally in terms of school and let him know that we are here to support him. If he needs a little tip and he's doing a paper and he comes and asks me, I'll help him out. *But I'm not going to go and ride him about it.* And I was riding him. . . . We have to lay off, just let him forget about [school] standards.

I can't help but wonder how these children's teachers would respond to these parents' *confessions.* Some would be sympathetic, I'm sure. Other teachers, however, might ask what kind of *message* these parents were sending to their children about the importance of education. I'm certain some teachers would question the judgment of parents who deliberately reduced the amount of time their children spent on schoolwork when common sense indicates these children, all of whom struggled in school, need to spend more time on school. My own sense is that these expressions of caring—and that's what I think they are— would be unintelligible to many educators. But the Springs, Thibaults, Moores, and Coopers wouldn't care what teachers thought about their judgments. Education is important to these parents, but so is their children's happiness and each was committed to making at least some effort to seeing that their children were not "miserable for six and a half hours" a day.

I also wonder what teachers made of Molly Reeves. Molly was not able to attend parent-teacher conferences because the state of Ohio required her to be in school (she was preparing for her high school equivalency exam) as a condition of public assistance. When her sons were in the early grades she was often unable to respond to written requests from the school because she couldn't read. Because she couldn't read she was, at times, unable to provide her children with the support they needed to complete their homework. It would have been easy for teachers to fall prey to stereotypes about single "welfare mothers" and urban Appalachians that attributed Joe and Steve Reeves' school troubles to their "home environment." Teachers wouldn't have known of her efforts to take her sons to the university reading clinic, how she scoured the "junk stores" to find books for her sons, how she struggled to learn to read so she could help her children with their schoolwork, or how she moved to a community where she felt isolated so her sons could go to what she hoped would be a supportive school. It would be easy to blame Molly Reeves and other mothers like her for their children's problems in school. It takes some effort—and, perhaps, faith—to recognize that Molly's kids are likely to fulfill her desire to do better economically than she has *because* she cares so deeply about her children and their education.

It's probably also difficult for school officials to recognize that behind the attack dog tactics of Cybil and Ralph Thorn is a passionate desire to do what's best for their children. It's probably just as hard to see the caring behind Michelle Phills' "neurotic" request to transfer her daughter to another classroom before she even met the teacher to whom her daughter had been assigned. Nor would it be hard to feel rejected by parents like the Coopers and McIsaacs who removed their children from public schools in favor of homeschooling.

The point here is not to cast aspersions on teachers. After all, I've been a teacher and I don't have particularly fond memories of aggressive and demanding parents like Michelle Phills or Ralph and Cybil Thorn. It is nearly impossible to have a congenial relationship with parents who choose to document each and every interaction with you in writing. However, analyzing my interviews has convinced me that, however it may appear to school officials, all of these parents care about their children and their children's schooling. And what is true of the parents I talked to is, I believe, true of almost all parents. Not all parents will be "nice" like Edna Bunker, nor do all parents have equal access to social, economic, and cultural resources to support their children's schooling. This does not alter what I think is a basic fact: It is a rare parent who is indifferent to the needs of his or her children and easy explanations of school failure that blame parents who do not care are unfair—or worse. Just because parents do not respond to school troubles as we would does not mean they don't care. It just means that they are not us and may not have our resources (Lareau 1989; Shockley et al. 1995).

"Everybody Is Not Fortunate."

It's amazing how many people know where to go and what to do and who to talk to.

—Interview with Cybil Thorn

I began this book by situating my interest in the effects of school trouble on the lives of families within the context of my own experience with my daughter, Anne's, struggles in school which, during her first seven years in school, frequently denied my wife, my children, and I the pleasures of family life. As I'm writing this chapter, Anne has just begun her junior year at the Lexington (Massachusetts) Waldorf School. At times she lacks dedication and she still loses the occasional assignment, but, overall, Anne is doing reasonably well in school. From time to time, we find ourselves nagging Anne about the importance of taking school seriously, but memories of the tensions and turmoil that plagued our family during the first seven years of Anne's schooling have begun to fade. It would, however, be a mistake to attribute Anne's turnaround to maturity, talent, or a "supportive" family—even though I believe all these things are true to some extent. Reflecting on the content of my interviews with parents has led me to acknowledge the degree to which privilege has been a factor in Anne's school success. When Anne was struggling with reading, she was fortunate to have had the support of a parent who had been a teacher and possessed some expertise in the teaching of reading. It could easily have been different. Anne was also able to resist placement in a special education program, in part, because she had parents who were able to use their influence with school officials to obtain some remedial support without having Anne labeled. When Anne's diminished self-esteem threatened her social and academic development, she was also fortunate that her parents had the financial resources to be able to send her to a relatively expensive private school which gave her the respect she needed to regain her self-esteem. Under other circumstances, circumstances over which Anne had no control, Anne's life may have worked out very differently. As a family, we were also lucky to have been able to draw on the support of friends, family, and, for a time, a family counselor, to help us manage the stresses of school trouble.

The children whose parents I interviewed also had the good fortune to have families who loved them very much. Parents did not, however, have equal access to various material resources they could bring to bear in support of their children's schooling. At the most obvious level, parents differed in terms of the financial resources they could draw on to support their children's schooling. "Expensive remedial help [and] independent testing" on top of private schooling may have required some "sacrifices" for Tanya Wallace and her husband, but these options weren't even a possibility for Celine Street, for example, who couldn't even afford a baby-sitter to get out of the house once a week or to Molly Reeves whose ability to buy food and pay the rent depended on public assistance. Similarly, the decision to homeschool their children significantly reduced the family incomes of the Coopers and the McIsaacs, but they were still able to meet their families' basic needs. Homeschooling was not, however, an option for single mothers like Betty Blake, Debbie Frick, or Maria Scott who were the sole providers for their families. As Mrs. Cooper herself acknowledged, "Everybody is not fortunate enough to do homeschooling."

"It's amazing how many people know where to go and what to do and who to talk to," Mrs. Thorn observed. But the Thorns were among those who had acquired extensive knowledge about "where to go" and "who to talk to." Their involvement in their sons' school and the school district's parent assembly helped them learn about the organization of the schools and also enabled them to cultivate relationships with district administrators and regional politicians they were able to draw upon to pressure teachers and principals to provide special education support for their children. Diane Riggs also used the relationships she developed when she volunteered at her children's school to get what she wanted from the school. Conversely, Molly Reeves berated herself because she didn't even know that parents could makes demands of schools.

> I was stupid. I didn't know nothin' about what parents could tell the principal. "Look, it's my kid and I know he can't read. Put him back." I didn't know this stuff. . . . Reading's got a lot to do with your knowing a lot of stuff.

But reading isn't the only factor in knowing "where to go [and] who to talk to." Janet Moore was able to locate help at the local university because she knew people who had this knowledge. "Everybody's a teacher in my family except me," she told me. Of course, some of the parents I interviewed were teachers, which gave them privileged access to knowledge they were able to use to influence schools and obtain useful services for their children. Recall how Tanya Wallace and Elma Kinkead, both teachers, used their knowledge of schools to have their high school-age daughters "labeled" as a means of getting access to services that would facilitate their daughters' admission to college and provide support for them once they were enrolled in universities. Many parents would probably not even know that there were advantages to having their children labeled so late in their school careers, much less how to initiate this process.

In general, knowledge is a resource many parents were able to use to support their children's schooling. Some parents knew what they could demand from the schools. They knew "where to go [and] who to talk to," while, again, Molly Reeves didn't even know she could make demands on schools. Molly was probably also disadvantaged in her relations with her sons' school by her own negative experiences in school. Celine Street observed that "a lot of people feel intimidated when they go and visit the principal" and I'm sure that's especially true for parents who had bad experiences when they were in school. School wasn't comfortable for Molly Reeves as a child and there is no reason to believe she was any more comfortable there as an adult, a feeling that Jeb Moore shared.

But even parents who had bad school experiences are at least familiar with the structures of schooling. Molly Reeves may have "learned nothin'" when she was in school as she claimed, but she did spend more than six years (more than 6000 hours) in a classroom. She knew something about the structure and the expectations of American schools. Immigrant parents like Millie Lau and Rachel Ng, however, didn't even have this advantage in their dealings with their children's schools. Mrs. Ng, for example, appreciated the de-emphasis on rote learning in North American schools compared to her own experience in Taiwanese schools. She even told me, through an interpreter, that her desire for less stressful schools was a factor in her family's move to Canada. But her unfamiliarity with more "child-centered" approaches to learning left her feeling helpless when it came to supporting her son's school work. Mrs. Lau, also from Taiwan, was even more baffled by the nature and content of her daughter, Bonnie's, schooling. To begin with, no one had ever satisfactorily explained to Mrs. Lau the meaning of Bonnie's "language problem" which Mrs. Lau mistakenly associated with learning English.

> They [school officials] don't say anything. They say, no, my daughter is in that [special] school, my daughter has a language problem. But my daughter has been in kindergarten, first grade, second grade, four years full days in school and my daughter still has a language problem.

Mrs. Lau believed that her daughter's "language problem" referred to Bonnie's learning of English, for which she held the school responsible. Nor did Mrs. Lau have much of a sense of what her daughter did in school all day except that she was disappointed the school didn't "push" her daughter as hard as Mrs. Lau wished. She also believed that her daughter was generally deficient in the reading, writing, and math skills appropriate for third grade, which was behind Mrs. Lau's emphasis on "mom's homework." Mrs. Lau tried to have her daughter moved out of the special school to her neighborhood school where she would learn more age-appropriate skills, but the school made this difficult for her by demanding that she first sign a form absolving the board of education of all responsibility for her daughter's learning. This perplexed and angered Mrs. Lau who had no idea how a "language problem" could affect her daughter's academic learning although she did observe that daughter worked "very slowly." When I asked Mrs. Lau if she had ever considered private schooling as an alternative she said, "no" because she (mistakenly) thought that the children in private schools must do "very, very well" academically. Bonnie's struggles in school were very hard on Mrs. Lau who told me that she'd "cried a thousand times" over her daughter's schooling. Differences in language, culture, and experience made it especially difficult for Mrs. Lau to cope with the emotional burdens of school trouble.

If we understand differences in language and culture as a disadvantage for parents like Millie Lau and Rachel Ng in their interactions with school personnel, then we can see that other parents are advantaged by English-speaking, middle-class backgrounds. After all, teachers are likely to establish congenial relations more readily with parents whose background and experience are similar to their own. In this way, language and social class are forms of "cultural capital" that parents can draw upon to facilitate relations with school officials as a means of influencing their children's education (Lareau 1989). Based on my interviews with single mothers, it would appear that marital status was also a kind of cultural capital some parents were able to draw on in their interactions with teachers and other school officials. Celine Street complained that schools "can't deal with parents who tell them what to do with their children" but, based on my interviews at least, it may be that teachers and principals have particular difficulty listening to single mothers. Because she reached this same conclusion, Betty Blake always took her friend Charles with her to meetings at her son's school so that she wouldn't get "pushed around." Charles was a resource single parents like Celine Street and Molly Reeves would have welcomed.

Listening to parents talk about their experiences with school troubles, it seems that there were also personal qualities some parents were able to draw on as a resource to mitigate the effects of school trouble. Michelle Phills required remarkable persistence, even audacity, to refuse to accept rejection as she sought the best services for her daughter in and out of the schools. A reading program at the local university, for example, turned her daughter down "five or six times" before finally accepting her into their program. But, as Michelle's husband noted, "Michelle doesn't listen to 'no.'" Similarly, the quality of the education Al and Ted Thorn received in school owed much to their parents dogged determination—"to dig in with [their] teeth. Drive you insane until [the school] do[es] something" as Mrs. Thorn put it. Other parents,

David Thibault and Betty Springs, for example, were not dispositionally suited to such tactics, however effective they might have been. Not every parent was able to be "nice" to teachers as Edna Bunker was, but all possessed personal qualities that affected their relations with their children's schools.

Finally, there were significant differences among the families I interviewed in the resources they were able to draw on to cope with the personal and interpersonal stresses of school trouble.

"I Pray a Lot."

My interview with single mother Celine Street lasted nearly two hours, the longest interview I had with any parent. It was clear to me that Celine needed someone to talk to. Her only time away from Dennis was on the commuter train each morning. She couldn't afford a baby-sitter which would have allowed her time without Dennis and her brothers and sisters wouldn't watch Dennis for her because they couldn't "control" him. Her sisters refused to be seen in public with Dennis which meant they wouldn't even go to the mall with Celine unless she could find someone to watch Dennis (which she couldn't). "My sisters won't even come shopping with me if I was there with Dennis because they get upset with his behavior in public," she told me. Celine's family, except for her mother who lived nearly a thousand miles away, wouldn't even talk with her about Dennis.

Celine Street has to bear the burden of school trouble alone. Most of the parents I talked to, however, had friends and family nearby who helped them cope with the emotional impact of school trouble on their lives. Maria Scott and her daughter, Tiffany, for example, lived with Maria's mother who often read books to Tiffany. Molly Reeves had brothers who lived near her who provided her with material and emotional support when she needed it. Betty Blake often drew on family friend Charles for comfort, advice, and support at school conferences. Jamie Frick had a several friends she talked to about her daughter's school trouble. Betty and Martin Springs, John and Alice Mandel, and Edna Bunker were among the parents who were able to take advantage of professional counselors to help their families deal with the emotional burdens of school trouble. Mothers and fathers in two-parent families always had each other to talk to even if not all fathers were equally supportive of their wives. Carol Dumay, for example, sometimes felt she had to talk to strangers on the bus about her daughter's struggles at school when her husband refused to listen to her concerns.

After feeling the pain of Celine Street's isolation, I was pleased to hear parents who were able to tell me about family and friends who were able to provide some comfort, but parents also told me about inner resources they drew upon when the stresses and tensions of school trouble threatened to overwhelm them. The Coopers, for example, impressed me with the degree to which their religious beliefs sustained them in times of stress. Here, for example, is how Mr. Cooper talked about the impact of homeschooling on their home finances.

> I'm praying that God will allow me to make it happen. Right now I'm pretty comfortable with where were at [financially]. And I think God is always opening doors and has blessed us . . . 'cause we did feel that the Lord guided us to do homeschooling.

But the Coopers also felt a need to repay this love by sharing what they had with a foster child.

> I guess in return God also said that there's enough love here for you to share with somebody else. So we've allowed a foster child to come into our home.

The Cooper's spiritual beliefs also gave them confidence in their ability to home school their children. Here's how Mrs. Cooper talked about her ability to take on the role of her children's teacher.

> It helps . . . knowing that you are capable because God tells me I'm capable because He gave me these children. I'm the first teacher they ever had and I can teach them any thing they need to know. So it's a spiritual thing to know that Jesus, He's with me and He's given me all that I need.

The Coopers acknowledged the stresses they'd experienced because of school trouble but, in their opinion, they were able to use prayer as a means of dealing with these tensions. Mr. Cooper described the role of prayer in his life this way. "I was praying to God just to show us the way that [He] wanted us to be able to handle [school trouble]," he said. Several other parents I interviewed also emphasized the role of prayer in helping them cope with their daughters' and sons' struggles in school. Betty Blake, for example, had this to say about her habit of praying for support and guidance.

> I pray that it's going to get better. I pray a lot. And the Lord answers my prayers, I'm a witness. Okay? And because of my spiritual background I tend not to let things upset me. . . . I don't think I could have pulled through this. Not only did I draw strength from the Lord and my family, they made me a stronger person and helped me get through this.

To some degree, every parent I interviewed referred to the emotional effects of school trouble on their families. Luckily, most parents were able to draw on family, friends, community resources, and their spiritual beliefs to sustain them when school troubles denied them some of the pleasures of parenthood. But, again, the material and emotional burdens of school trouble fell most heavily on single mothers, who had the most difficulty getting the support they needed to sustain them during periods of stress.

In our culture, school success is linked to individual ability and supportive families. My interviews indicate that capable children with caring parents can still struggle in school although some parents are able to bring to bear various resources that can at least soften the effects of school trouble on their children and their families. In this sense, school success and failure may be less about "survival of the fittest" than "survival of the luckiest" and, to the degree that financial resources, knowledge, and other forms of cultural capital mitigate the effects of school trouble, some children are luckier than others.

Parents Denied: The Effects of School Troubles on the Lives of Families

In the final section of this book, I'd like to reiterate some of the major themes that emerged from my interviews with parents and consider how parents and teachers might think about some of the issues that emerged from this research project.

I began with a curiosity about how parents of children who struggled in school experience their children's schooling. Would school trouble disrupt roles and relationships in these families as it had in my family, denying these parents many of the pleasures of parenthood? My interviews indicate that, at least among the parents I spoke to, school trouble—even relatively minor trouble at school—threatens the happiness and self-esteem of children for whom school is a struggle, disrupts relationships between husbands and wives, parents and children, and among siblings, and, in general, denies families many of the pleasures of family life. Hours spent on homework, for example, limit opportunities for families to celebrate their relationships by taking a family bike ride, walking in the park, or just going "fishin.'" School trouble distorts family relationships by focusing parents' interactions with the child who struggles in school on their deficiencies. Tensions over schoolwork and the fixation of their parents' attention on *problems* caused many children to doubt their parents' love. The intrusion of school troubles in the lives of families also reduces parents' opportunities to interact with children who do relatively well in school. School trouble leads parents to minimize the achievements of the *other* children for fear of making the child who struggles in school "feel worse." To the degree that the *other* children feel marginalized, they may harbor resentment toward their struggling sibling and toward parents who fail to give them the attention they feel they deserve. Some fathers also resented the inordinate amount of time their wives spent attending to school trouble—and not to them. In general, the intrusion of school trouble into the lives of the parents I interviewed created an atmosphere in which *family values* were subverted by values of schooling.

Of course, the weight of school trouble fell unevenly within the families to whom I spoke and, in general, mothers endured a disproportionate share of the emotional and material burdens of their children's struggles at school. And, among mothers, single mothers had to cope with school trouble on their own. These women bore the sole responsibility for the financial, domestic, and emotional needs of their families and these duties were exacerbated by the exigencies of school trouble. And while school trouble often complicated already complex relations between parents and their children's school, single mothers' relations with school officials were further complicated by their sense that teachers and principals took them less seriously because of their status as single mothers.

School troubles also engaged parents in more frequent and intense interactions with their children's schools and, perhaps because the focus of these interactions was negative, the relations between these parents and their children's schools were often tense and stressful. But there was never any doubt that these parents cared deeply about their children's education and were prepared to do whatever they *could* to support their children's schooling.

The parents I interviewed made it clear that school trouble affected the quality of their family lives. Some parents were, however, able to draw on various financial, community, emotional, spiritual, and *cultural* resources that mitigated the effects of school trouble. But parents did not have equal access to these resources, which meant that effects of school trouble were more painful for some families than others, but this was undeserved unless you believe that people are to blame for being poor, working class, less educated, or unmarried, for example, which I do not. But, regardless of parents' backgrounds, their access to material and cultural resources, or the nature of their children's "problem," the parents I interviewed cared deeply about their children's education and their overall well-being even if expressions of caring were not easily intelligible to school officials.

What should we make of the stories of school troubles these parents were kind enough to share with me? While I readily acknowledge that not everyone will have the same reading of this text, the following are some of my own impressions of what can be learned from the stories these parents had to tell, and my advice to teachers.

Begin with the Assumption That Parents Care

It is easy, but unfair, to blame school failure on uncaring parents. My interviews indicate strongly that caring, supportive parents can still have children who struggle in school. My interviews also suggest that—however it may seem to some teachers—uncaring parents are probably rare. Parents do differ in terms of the resources they are able to bring to bear in support of their children's schooling, but it would not be fair to fault parents for their inability to pay for private testing or tutoring, for example. Nor would it be fair to blame students' school trouble on uninvolved parents based on traditional measures of parent involvement such as attending teacher-parent conferences or surveiling children's homework. Not all parents can easily attend school conferences, nor are all parents equally comfortable in school and, as my interviews indicate, parents can deliberately ignore the demands of schooling *because* they care. There seems to be general agreement that parent involvement is an important ingredient for any version of school reform. However, there is little chance for improved relations between schools and parents if teachers and other school officials begin with the assumption that parents don't care about their children.

Collaborative Relationships Begin with Trust

It may be that there is a natural tension between parents and their children's teachers, as Sara Lawrence Lightfoot argues. If so, these tense relationships can easily be exacerbated by school troubles. For many of the parents I interviewed, congenial relations with their children's teachers depended on expressions of caring from teachers. Parents acknowledged the often overwhelming demands on teachers, but still expected teachers to recognize their children's *specialness* by providing instruction appropriate to their needs and abilities, recognizing their children's strengths as well as weaknesses, and, above all, treating their children with respect. Meeting the challenges of students who struggle in school depends, I believe, on the collaborative efforts of parents and teachers, but the ability to develop these collaborative relationships depends on the development of trust (Edwards 1999). Trust, in turn, will develop only when parents feel that they and their children are being treated with respect. And a key to showing respect is beginning with the assumption that *all* parents care deeply about their children and their children's education.

Broaden Notions of Parent Involvement

There seems to be considerable support for the assertion that parents ought to be involved in their children's schooling. There is also some agreement among educators that parent involvement is especially desirable when children struggle in school. I do not disagree. As a former special education teacher, I know how much parents of students with special needs want to be connected to their children's schooling and how helpful it can be when they are involved. However, as many of my interviews show, school trouble causes considerable stress in many families and parent involvement in their children's schooling can increase that stress. The tensions around homework, for example, did significant harm to some families, and children often resented parents' efforts to surveil their schoolwork. Amy Thibault and Catherine Connor protected their relationships with their sons by turning responsibility for their children's schoolwork over to their husbands, an option that was not available to most mothers. Most parents, because they cared about their children's education, continued to endure the tensions of homework despite the harm it was doing to their relationships with their children. Given the demands of schooling, it was difficult for these parents to find a way to disengage themselves from these tense, unsatisfying interactions with their children. Perhaps school homework policies should be revised so that they are considerate of the emotional needs of families. I'm sure many people would agree with Newt Gingrich, former Speaker of the U.S. House of Representatives, that children who don't have at least two hours of homework per night are "being cheated for the rest of their lives." However, my interviews suggest that these demands may do irreparable harm to the emotional life of many families, in particular families with children for whom school is a struggle. So, in some cases, less parent involvement in children's schooling may be the best course or, at a minimum, teachers should talk to parents about how they'd like to be involved in their children's education (see Edwards 1999 for guidance on how to conduct interviews with parents).

Many of the parents I interviewed were anxious to be involved in their children's school, but were unwilling to accept versions of parent involvement in which they did not have an active voice in their children's education. These parents desired collaborative relationships with schools but their overtures for collaboration were often rejected by teachers and principals who preferred parents who limited their *involvement* to expressions of support for the school's agenda. Parent involvement negotiated solely on schools' terms will never be acceptable to parents like Jamie Frick and Alice Mandel. Teachers who believe that parents should play an active role in their children's education must find ways to accommodate parents like Jamie and Alice.

Develop More Flexible Homework Policies

As I documented in Chapter 4, homework is a particularly stressful presence in the homes where there is a child who struggles in school. Homework can negatively affect relationships between parents and their children and between wives and husbands. Creating flexible homework policies that seek to reduce these stresses may not be so easy, however. One obvious remedy to the homework problem is to assign less homework to students for whom school is a struggle. Alternatively, teachers could define homework in terms of the amount of time spent on school work (e.g., thirty minutes) instead of the amount of work to be completed (e.g., four pages of math). Many parents, however, may resist this compromise if they suspect it involves lowering short-term academic expectations that affect their long-term aspirations for their children. Homework policies also need to be considerate of the ability of parents to support their children's homework. In either case, the only way to develop appropriate homework policies that are sensitive to the needs individual families is by talking candidly with parents about homework—specifically, how teachers and parents can work together to support children's schoolwork without seriously upsetting family relationships.

What I learned from those interviews also suggests some advice for parents.

Take Comfort in the Stories of Other Parents

I hope other parents of children who struggle in school can take some comfort from the stories of the parents I interviewed. School trouble is disruptive on the lives and relationships of families, and parents of children for whom school is a struggle might want to focus at least as much energy on finding ways to reduce the tensions that derive from school trouble as they do supporting their children's academic needs. The support of a professional counselor, if available, can be helpful. It may also be useful to take the example of parents like David Thibault and John Cooper to find ways to relieve tension around schoolwork even if it means sometimes ignoring the demands of schooling. School is important, but not so important that it is worth sacrificing lifelong relationships with our children.

Teachers Care

Just as it's unfair to conclude that children fail in school because their parents don't care, it is also unfair to conclude that children fail because their teachers don't care. The parents I spoke to had their share of horror stories about uncaring or indifferent teachers. I've had similar experiences. Still, the vast majority of teachers I work with—and I have had the good fortune to work with teachers across the United States and Canada—are good, caring people. That's why they went into teaching in the first place. Many teachers are demoralized by all the teacher bashing that's occurring in the media and legislatures across North America. They're frustrated by prescriptive curricula and high stakes testing that make it increasingly difficult to attend to the needs of individual children. So, while I would encourage all parents to be their child's advocate, I would also encourage them to take Edna Bunker's example and be "nice." Teachers besieged by angry and hostile parents will have difficulty creating a warm, caring, and respectful environment for their students. After all, it is hard to offer respect if you don't get any yourself. The only excuse for being unkind to a teacher is if that teacher has been deliberately unkind to our children—a rare event, I think.

Demand What's Best for Children

Recall how Molly Reeves berated herself for not recognizing that she could make demands on schools. I think all parents of students who struggle in school should take Molly's example and be willing to make (reasonable) demands on schools on behalf of their children. I'm not sure it's reasonable to request a change of teachers based on a one-minute observation, as Michelle Phills did. It is more than reasonable to request a change of teachers if that teacher fails to treat students with respect or cannot recognize their special qualities, however. And if some parents can demand more homework for their children, as I'm told some parents do, then it is just as reasonable—perhaps even *more* reasonable—to request less homework when homework is destroying our relationships with our children. And, I think every parent should be able to ask their child's teacher: "What are you doing to challenge my child to do her or his best work?" I'm sure most parents of struggling students would agree with me: I don't care how my children compare to other children in their class or in other classes, in other schools, or in other states. I want to know how my children are doing in terms of their own abilities. I want to know that my son and daughter are being challenged, that they're being supported, that they're being respected, and, most of all, that they're happy. I also think it's reasonable to request that schools work with us if our children are "miserable for six and a half hours a day" to change that situation.

Seek Support

My interviews indicate that parents did not have equal access to the range of resources that could support them and their children. Some discovered university reading clinics that offered good reading programs for their children at minimal cost, for example. Others discovered they had the freedom to change schools in search of teachers, schools, and programs more congenial to their children's needs. Some parents knew not only that they could request particular teachers, but knew which teachers to request. My advice is that every parent make every effort to identify the resources that are available to them by asking friends and calling community agencies (e.g., the local Association for Children and Adults with Learning Disabilities) and the local college or university.

Resist Educational Reforms That Fail to Respect Children

Finally, parents and teachers—and anyone else interested in schooling—should wonder why we've created schools that make so many children and their families "miserable" for such a significant portion of their lives. Why, in the service of fiscal restraint, do we accept huge classes that make it nearly impossible for teachers to recognize and support our children's special qualities? If we put thirty to forty dogs in a space as small as the average classroom for "six and a half hours a day," I have no doubt there would be a public outcry. Why do we quietly accept the claims of politicians that "class size doesn't matter?"

Why do we accept increasingly narrow curricula—that is, more emphasis on the "basics" at the expense of art, music, and physical education programs—that reduce children's opportunities to display their competence? Who is advantaged and disadvantaged by these practices?

Why do we vote for politicians who push "higher standards" that, in reality, demand more failure as a means of affirming the successes of the highest achievers? And, finally, why do we accept educational reforms that turn schools into harsh, pressure-packed, heartless learning factories and attempt to reshape families in the image of schools?

In the short term, teachers and parents should work together to create ways of mitigating the effects of school failure. In the long term, parents and teachers should collaborate on challenging structures of schooling that produce so much failure in the first place. We can create schools that are academically demanding *and* respectful of children's humanity. We should do this because we care.

Epilogue: Anne

After I completed the final draft of this book, I asked Anne, my daughter, to read the first chapter. I wanted her feedback on the accuracy of events in her life that are recounted there but, more than that, I hoped for her explicit approval to share potentially embarrassing details about her life in school. And I was interested in her response as a reader.

Anne took to this task immediately. In fact, over the next day or so she read the chapter three times, sharing parts of it with a boyfriend. Overall, Anne felt that my descriptions of her struggles in school were accurate. She granted her permission for me to share details of her struggles in school with my readers, but she wanted me to know that the memories stirred up by reading this chapter were painful for her. "It made me cry," she confessed. Frankly, it hurt me to discover how raw these memories still were for her. Anne also shared with me her opinion that the chapter "read well," but—and this was a big but—she was embarrassed that "everyone will read that I had trouble with trigonometry and logarithms. People will think I'm stupid." Leaving aside the accuracy of her assertion that "everyone" will be reading this book, I tried to offer Anne a rationale for including these "embarrassing" details. "I want to avoid a Disney-esque, 'everyone lived happily after' ending to your story," I explained. "I understand," she told me, "but I did really well this year in lots of stuff. I have lots of friends." Anne then dug a civics assignment out of her backpack on which her teacher had written "excellent" to help make her case. "What if I write a brief epilogue that summarizes some of your accomplishments?" I asked her. She agreed.

Last spring, Anne completed her sophomore year at the Lexington Waldorf High School. She passed all of her courses (everything is pass-fail) and received several "pass with distinctions." Late in the year, she got 100 percent on a test on the *Grapes of Wrath* in her English course. In math, she still exhibits test anxiety but, overall, Anne is growing into a confident young woman. She has lots of friends. She (finally) speaks in class. She did a wonderful job performing in her class play—she played the part of Mrs. Candour in Sheridan's *School for Scandal*. Perhaps the best evidence of Anne's growing confidence is that, as this book goes to press, Anne is in the middle of a semester-long exchange at the

Waldorf High School in Lima, Peru. Last summer Anne worked as a counselor at a Montessori day camp and did so well that she has already been invited back for next summer. I'm hopeful about Anne's future, but I'll never forget the pain and frustration of her early years in school. I'm pleased things seem to be going well for Anne but I'll never get over the feeling that, if it wasn't for school troubles, our lives would have been—well, maybe not perfect, but much, much better.

References

Allington, R. L. 1980. "Poor Readers Don't Get to Read Much in Reading Groups." *Language Arts* 57: 872–876.

Allington, R. L., and A. McGill-Franzen. 1989. "Different Programs, Indifferent Instruction." In *Beyond Special Education: Quality Education for All* edited by D. K. Lipsky and A. Gartner. Baltimore, MD: Paul H. Brookes Publishing.

Baker, D. P., and D. L. Stevenson. 1986. "Mothers' Strategies for Children's School Achievement: Managing the Transition to High School." *Sociology of Education* 59: 156–166.

Barlow, M., and H. J. Robertson. 1994. *Class Warfare: The Assault on Canada's Schools*. Toronto, ONT: Key Porter.

Begley, S. 1998. "Homework Doesn't Help." *Newsweek* 131 13: 50–51.

Berliner, D., and B. Biddle. 1995. *The Manufactured Crisis: Myths, Frauds, and the Attack on America's Public Schools*. New York: Addison-Wesley.

Black, S. 1996. "The Truth About Homework." *American School Board Journal* 183 (10): 48–51.

Callahan, K., J. A. Rademacher, and B. L. Hildreth. 1998. "The Effect of Parent Participation in Strategies to Improve the Homework Performance of Students Who Are At Risk." *Remedial and Special Education* 19: 131–41.

Canter, L., and L. Hausner. 1988. *Homework Without Tears*. New York: Perennial Library.

Carbo, M. 1978. "Teaching Reading with Talking Books." *The Reading Teacher* 32: 267–273.

Chomsky, C. 1976. "After Decoding What?" *Language Arts* 53: 288–296.

Cooper, H. 1989. "Synthesis of Research on Homework." *Educational Leadership* 47 (3): 85–91.

Dudley-Marling, C. C. 1997. *Living with Uncertainty: The Messy Reality of Classroom Practice*. Portsmouth, NH: Heinemann.

Dudley-Marling, C. C., and R. R. Rosenberg. 1984. *Parent Involvement in the Interdisciplinary Team Process*. Denver: University of Colorado. (ERIC Document Reproduction Service No. ED 235 670.

Edwards, P. 1999. *A Path to Follow*. Portsmouth, NH: Heinemann.

Gardner, H. 1983. *Frames of Mind: The Theory of Multiple Intelligences*. New York: Basic Books.

Gee, J. P. 1990. *Social Linguistics and Literacies: Ideology in Discourses*. Bristol, PA: Falmer Press.

Glass, G. V. 1983. "Effectiveness of Special Education." *Policy Studies Review* 2: 65–78.

Glasser, W. 1975. *Schools Without Failure*. New York: Harper and Row.

Green, R. 1995. "High Achievement, Underachievement, and Learning Disabilities." In *The Family-School Connection: Theory, Research, Practice*, edited by B. A. Ryan, B. R. Adams, T. P. Gullotta, R. P. Weissberg, and R. L. Hampton. Thousand Oaks, CA: Sage.

Griffith, A. I. October, 1996. *A Chorus of Voices: Mothers in Schools*. Paper presented at the Popular feminism lectures, Center for Women's Studies in Education, University of Toronto, Toronto, Canada.

Griffith, A. I., and D. E. Smith. 1990. "'What Did You Do in School Today?': Mothering, Schooling, and Social Class." In *Perspectives on Social Problems*, Vol. 2., edited by G. Miller and J. A. Holstein. Greenwich, CT: JAI Press.

Heath, S. B. 1983. *Ways with Words: Language, Life, and Work in Communities and Classrooms*. New York: Cambridge University Press.

Kingsolver, B. 1995. *High Tide in Tucson: Essays from Now or Never*. New York: HarperCollins.

Lareau, A. 1989. *Home Advantage: Social Class and Parental Intervention in Elementary Education*. New York: Falmer Press.

———. 1992. "It's More Covert Today: The Importance of Race in Shaping Parents' Views of the School." In *Schooling and the Silenced "Others": Race and Class in Schools*, edited by L. Weiss, M. Fine, and A. Lareau. Buffalo: Graduate School of Education Publications, Buffalo Research Institute on Education for Teaching, State University of New York at Buffalo.

Lightfoot, S. 1978. *Worlds Apart: Relationships Between Families and Schools*. New York: Basic Books.

Madaus, G. F. 1988. "The Influence of Testing on the Curriculum." In *Critical Issues in Curriculum. Eighty-seventh yearbook of the National Society for the Study of Education—Part I*, edited by L. N. Tanner. Chicago: University of Chicago Press.

Maslow, A. 1954. *Motivation and Personality*. New York: Harper.

McDermott, R. 1993. "The Acquisition of a Child by a Learning Disability." In *Understanding Practice*, edited by S. Chaiklin and J. Lave. New York: Cambridge University Press.

McDermott, R. P., S. V. Goldman, and H. Varenne. 1984. "When School Goes Home: Some Problems in the Organization of Homework." *Teachers College Record* 85: 391–409.

Miller, L. 1993. *What We Call Smart: A New Narrative for Intelligence and Learning*. San Diego, CA: Singular Publishing.

Ohanian, S. 1999. *One Size Fits Few*. Portsmouth, NH: Heinemann.

Parkay, F. W., and W. M. Bartnick. 1991. "A Comparative Analysis of the 'Holding' Power of General and Exceptional Education." *Remedial and Special Education* 12: 17–22.

Parlardy, J. M. 1995. "Another Look at Homework." *Principal* 74: 32–33.

Purcell-Gates, V. 1995. *Other People's Words: The Cycle of Low Literacy.* Cambridge, MA: Harvard University Press.

Radencich, M., and J. S. Schumm. 1988. *How to Help Your Child with Homework: Every Caring Parent's Guide to Encouraging Good Study Habits and Ending the Homework Wars: For Parents of Children Ages 6–13.* Minneapolis, MN: Free Spirit.

Rasinski, T. 1989. "Fluency for Everyone: Incorporating Fluency Instruction in the Classroom." *The Reading Teacher* 42: 690–693.

Rhodes, L. K. 1981. "I Can Read! Predicable Books as Resources for Reading and Writing Instruction." *The Reading Teacher* 34: 511–518.

Rhodes, L. K., and C. Dudley-Marling. 1996. *Readers and Writers with a Difference: A Holistic Approach to Teaching Struggling Students.* 2d ed. Portsmouth, NH: Heinemann.

Rist, R. C. 1970. "Student Social Class and Teacher Expectations: The Self-Fulfilling Prophecy in Ghetto Education." *Harvard Educational Review* 40: 411–451.

Rosemond, J. K. 1990. *Ending the Homework Hassle: Understanding, Preventing, and Solving School Performance Problems.* Kansas City, MO: Andrews and McMeel.

Salend, S. J., and M. Gajria. 1995. "Increasing the Homework Completion Rates of Students with Mild Disabilities." *Remedial and Special Education* 16: 271–78.

Shockley, B., B. Michalove, and J. Allen. 1995. *Engaging Families: Connecting Home and School Literacy Communities.* Portsmouth, NH: Heinemann.

Skrtic, T. M. 1991. *Behind Special Education: A Critical Analysis of Professional Culture and School Organization.* Denver, CO: Love.

Smith, C. R. 1986. "The Future of the LD Field: Intervention Approach." *Journal of Learning Disabilities* 19, 461–472.

Smith, F. 1998. *The Book of Learning and Forgetting.* New York: Teachers College Press.

Smith, M. 1980. "Meta-Analyses of Research on Teacher Expectation." *Evaluation in Education* 4: 53–55.

Spring, J. 1997. *Political Agendas for Education: From the Christian Coalition to the Green Party.* Mahwah, NJ: Lawrence Erlbaum.

Stevenson, D. L., and D. P. Baker. 1987. "The Family-School Relation and the Child's School Performance." *Child Development* 58: 1348–57.

Taylor, D. 1991. *Literacy Denied.* Portsmouth, NH: Heinemann.

Turnbull, A. P., and H. R. Turnbull. 1986. *Families, Professionals and Exceptionality: A Special Partnership.* Columbus: Charles Merrill.

Uhrmacher, P. B. 1995. "Uncommon Schooling: A Historical Look at Rudolph Steiner, Anthroposophy, and Waldorf Education." *Curriculum Inquiry* 25: 381–406.

U.S. Department of Education. 1987. *What Works: Research About Teaching and Learning.* 2d ed. Washington, DC: U.S. Department of Education.

Valdes, G. 1996. *Con Respeto: Bridging the Distance Between Culturally Diverse Families and Schools—An Ethnographic Portrait.* New York: Teachers College Press.

Walberg, H. J. 1991. "Does Homework Help?" *School Community Journal* 1 (1): 13–15.

Weiss, R. S. 1995. *Learning from Strangers: The Art and Method of Qualitative Interview Studies.* New York: Free Press.

Wien, C. A., and C. Dudley-Marling. 1998. "Limited Vision: The Ontario Curriculum and Outcomes-Based Education." *Canadian Journal of Education* 23: 405–420.